T0012849

THE
GEEKY
CHEF
COOKBOOK

THE
GEEKY
CHEF

REAL-LIFE RECIPES  FOR FANTASY FOODS

COOKBOOK

CASSANDRA REEDER, THE GEEKY CHEF

Race Point
PUBLISHING

Inspiring | Educating | Creating | Entertaining

Brimming with creative inspiration, how-to projects, and useful information to enrich your everyday life, quarto.com is a favorite destination for those pursuing their interests and passions.

Text © 2015 and 2017 by Cassandra Reeder
Photography © 2015 and 2017 by Quarto Publishing Group USA Inc. (pp. 97, 101, and 105 © Jeffrey Diza)

This edition published in 2020 by Race Point Publishing, an imprint of The Quarto Group,
142 West 36th Street, 4th Floor, New York, NY 10018, USA
T (212) 779-4972 F (212) 779-6058 www.Quarto.com

First published in 2015 as *The Geeky Chef Cookbook* and includes recipes from *The Geeky Chef Strikes Back* (2017) by Race Point Publishing, an imprint of The Quarto Group, 142 West 36th Street, 4th Floor, New York, NY 10018.

Race Point titles are also available at discount for retail, wholesale, promotional and bulk purchase. For details, contact the Special Sales Manager by email at specialsales@quarto.com or by mail at The Quarto Group, Attn: Special Sales Manager, 100 Cummings Center Suite, 265D, Beverly, MA 01915, USA.

10 9 8 7 6

ISBN: 978-1-63106-710-5

Library of Congress Control Number:2019957373

Publisher: Rage Kindelsperger
Creative Director: Laura Drew
Editorial Project Manager: Leeann Moreau
Managing Editor: Cara Donaldson
Senior Editor: Erin Canning
Cover and Interior Design: Amelia LeBarron
Photography: Bill Milne
Food Styling: Noah Rosenbaum and Kristy Hollidge
Illustration (p. 8): Denis Caron

Printed in China

CONTENTS

69
MAIN DISHES

103
CAKES AND CUPCAKES

131
OTHER DESSERTS

INTRODUCTION

So, you're a geek, a nerd, a neo-maxi-zoom-dweebie. Or, you know, maybe you don't like labels and you're just really into sci-fi. That's cool. I'm just guessing here, but you probably also like to eat. Great! Then this book is for you. Generally, the kind of people who acquire the labels listed above, in addition to being wicked smart and perhaps experiencing a certain amount of social discomfort, tend to have a passion for a piece of work that consumes them. My blog, *The Geeky Chef*, was the love child of that intense nerd passion and my fondness for cooking.

Really, I have always had a fascination with food in fiction. When I was six years old, I enlisted my big brother to help me make Tree Star cookies after watching Don Bluth's *The Land Before Time*. I also made Unicorn Hair Soup after reading the wonderful YA novel *Ella Enchanted* when I was slightly older. I could really go on and on with these examples, but the tipping point that inspired *The Geeky Chef* actually started with a *Zelda* game.

It was a dark and stormy winter night in San Francisco. No, really! I'm not making that up for atmosphere. The year was 2008. My then-boyfriend (now husband) and I were playing *The Legend of Zelda: Twilight Princess*. In case you were wondering, we are able to play single-player games together because we have developed a system where I do the puzzles and he fights the bosses, which is not unlike how we handle most obstacles in real life. The level we were on was called the Snowpeak Ruins, which is basically this giant abandoned mansion occupied by two yetis. To complete this part of the game, Link must collect ingredients to make a soup to heal the female yeti. The ingredients are a fish, a pumpkin, and goat cheese. When you successfully locate all of these items and add them to the soup, you get a consumable called Superb Soup. At that point in time, my husband and I had been living almost exclusively on ramen and cereal, so maybe it was malnourishment speaking, but that soup sounded so good to me. I decided as a special treat that I was going to make Yeto's Superb Soup for Thanksgiving.

So, I hit up the old search engines looking for a recipe, fully expecting someone to have thought of this already. The game was a couple of years old at that point, but, alas, to my surprise and disappointment, there was nothing. At that time, the Internet wasn't quite what it is now, and though there were some sites with fiction-inspired recipes, they were mostly dedicated to something specific: primarily *Harry Potter* and *The Lord of the Rings*. So, I decided that a) I was going to scratch my own itch and make the website I was looking for, and b) I was totally going to make my own recipe for Yeto's Superb Soup. In the end, this worked out pretty well for me.

Now my humble little blog has its own cookbook. This still sorta blows my mind, and I have you guys to thank for it. Thank you to everyone who buys this book, and thank you to every nerd who stumbled on my blog while searching for a Lembas recipe, and thank you for every suggestion that helped me discover new geeky things to love. All of you made one of my biggest dreams come true.

As a little girl, I always expected that one day adventure would happen to me—someday a tornado would whisk me away to Oz, or I'd fall down a rabbit hole, or David Bowie would kidnap me and take me to his labyrinth where he'd sing me songs and feed me magic peaches. As I get older, I realize you have to make adventure happen for yourself. I hope this cookbook helps you, dear reader, to make some tasty adventures for yourself—and maybe throw some really awesome LARP parties.

And if you happen to be the architect behind any of the works that inspired these recipes: Hi, I love you, please don't sue me! I am a fan, and my goal here is to help other fans enjoy your work even more by giving them a taste of your imagination. I rather hope that this book will help people to discover new geeky things to love, as writing this book has done for me.

A NOTE ON COOKING
AND INGREDIENTS

Cooking is like an adventure: there's an end goal in mind but it is the journey that makes the end meaningful. You'll notice that I leave a lot of room for choices and that some of the ingredients have ranged amounts. This is because I want to encourage you to follow your own instincts when cooking. If you think you need fewer people in your Soylent Green, try it! Make substitutions, add the ingredients you wish were there, include more of this and less of that. Cooking is rarely a precise science, and it's adding your individual touch that makes the food good. I guess what I'm saying is play with your food! Experimentation is how you learn and grow. When in doubt, Google or YouTube it!

Due to the nature of this book, some of the ingredients are a little "out there," as we're dealing in the realms of science fiction and fantasy. I've tried to limit rare ingredients and supplies needed as much as possible. With a few exceptions, most of the ingredients and supplies can be found at any generic grocery store. Those that can't, can be found through online vendors.

BASIC PREP RECIPES

THE SPICES MUST FLOW

I like to use a lot of herbs and spices. If a recipe calls for two cloves of garlic, I put in about seven. Because of this, I am somewhat reluctant to add measurements for seasoning and spice. Just think of the seasoning amounts as suggestions, and follow your heart and your taste buds.

I'm including two of my go-to seasoning blends that I use in much of my cooking and baking, and which will appear in many of these recipes. You may think that mixing a spice blend is just making things unnecessarily complicated, but premixing spice and seasoning blends actually saves you a ton of time in the long run. Instead of having to individually dole out each spice, you will have it all ready to go in just one bottle.

These are a couple of basics to start you off; I highly recommend experimenting with your own seasoning blends as they're definitely one of the most useful things to have in the kitchen. You'll be amazed at the depth of flavor you can develop when you start mixing and matching your own spice blends. Bonus: You'll feel like an alchemist or a wizard with all the bottles and jars of stuff.

ALL-PURPOSE SAVORY SEASONING BLEND

3 parts garlic powder
3 parts onion powder
2 parts dried parsley
1 part sea salt
1 part ground black pepper

ALL-PURPOSE SWEET SPICE BLEND
(AKA SPICE MÉLANGE)

4 parts ground cinnamon
1 part ground allspice
1 part ground nutmeg
1 part ground cloves
1 part ground ginger

PREPARE TO PIE

Pie dough is intimidating and, honestly, sometimes buying a premade one from the store is totally worth it. However, if you are willing to spend the time and energy to make a superior homemade crust, this recipe will do the trick.

SINGLE CRUST
(MAKES DOUGH FOR 1 SINGLE-CRUST PIE)

1¼ cups (155 g) all-purpose flour
1 teaspoon granulated sugar (optional)
Generous pinch salt
½ cup or 1 stick (120 g) unsalted butter, chilled
3 tablespoons ice water
Makes dough for 1 single-crust pie.

DOUBLE CRUST
(MAKES DOUGH FOR 1 DOUBLE-CRUST PIE)

2½ cups (310 g) all-purpose flour
2 teaspoons granulated sugar (optional)
¾ teaspoons salt
1 cup or 2 sticks (240 g) unsalted butter, chilled
6 tablespoons ice water

1. Mix the flour, sugar, and salt in a food processor. Slice the butter into the processor and pulse everything until it forms crumbs. Blend in enough ice water to create moist clumps, but not so it is all stuck together.

2. Gather the dough into a ball with your hands. If you're making double crust, divide the dough in half and form into 2 balls. Flatten into disc(s), wrap in plastic wrap and chill for at least 2 hours.

THE YELLOW CAKE IS NOT A LIE

Or, it doesn't have to be. You can be enjoying some cake with your companion cube in about 40 minutes. With some modifications, you can use the yellow cake recipe as the base for many cakes. It's pretty magical.

1 cup or 2 sticks (240 g) unsalted butter, softened
1½ cups (300 g) granulated sugar
2 eggs, separated
2 teaspoons vanilla extract
2 cups (250 g) cake flour
1 tablespoon baking powder
1 teaspoon baking soda
1 teaspoon salt
1 cup (240 ml) buttermilk

1. Preheat the oven to 325°F (170°C).
2. In a large bowl, cream together the butter and sugar. Add in the egg yolks and the vanilla, mixing until fully incorporated. Set aside.
3. In a separate bowl, combine the flour, baking powder, baking soda, and salt.
4. Gradually sprinkle the dry ingredients into the wet ingredients and stir, alternating with the buttermilk.
5. Mix until the batter is fluffy, but be careful not to overmix.
6. In a separate bowl, beat the egg whites until they are foamy and thick.
7. Very gently fold the egg whites into the batter and mix until incorporated. Again, do not overmix.
8. Transfer to two 9-inch (23 cm) cake pans, ramekins, or two 6-cup muffin/cupcake tins.
9. Bake for 30–35 minutes for the two 9-inch (23 cm) cake pans, 20–25 minutes for cupcakes or ramekins, or until a toothpick inserted in the center of a cake comes out clean.

SNACKS, APPETIZERS, AND SIDES

FIGGINS

MAKES 9 FIGGINS

Terry Pratchett's wacky and hilarious series contains a lot of edible things, though many are not entirely appealing. Pig's ear soup, anyone? How about some rat fruit? No? But if you're a *Discworld* fan, I highly recommend purchasing *Nanny Ogg's Cookbook*.

Other than a mysterious word for an unknown body part from which one would not want to be hung, a Figgin is defined in *Guards! Guards!* as a shortcrust pastry containing raisins or, alternately, in Interesting Times as a small bun with currants in it. I made a *Guards! Guards!* version. I also included figs, because, you know, FIG-gins.

INGREDIENTS

DOUGH
¾ cup or 1½ sticks (180 g) butter
2 cups (240 g) flour
Ice water

FILLING
¾ cup (110 g) raisins
¼ cup (35 g) chopped dried figs
½ cup (120 ml) orange juice
¼ cup (60 ml) honey, or to taste
1 teaspoon orange zest
1 teaspoon allspice
1 teaspoon ground cinnamon
Pinch ground ginger
¼ cup or ½ stick (60 g) butter

1. **To make the dough:** In a large bowl, add the flour with the ¾ cup (180 g) of butter. Using your fingers, work the butter into the flour until you have a crumbly texture. Add a tiny amount of ice water to the flour and butter and combine until the dough is very stiff.

2. Cover the dough and place in the fridge while you make the filling.

3. **To make the filling:** Put the raisins, figs, orange juice, honey, zest, spices, and the ¼ cup (60 g) of butter into a saucepan and simmer for 10 to 15 minutes. If any liquid remains, discard it. Leave to cool.

4. Preheat the oven to 375°F (190°C). Divide the dough into 9 even pieces. Roll out each piece until it is ⅛ inch (3 mm) thick, then use a tea saucer as a template and cut around it with a knife.

5. Spoon about a tablespoon of the filling into the center of a circle, then pull the dough edges into the center of the circle over the filling and press together. Note: Wet your fingers slightly with cold milk or water when doing this to ensure the edges seal. When sealed, use your hands or a roller to flatten the Figgin a bit.

6. Flip the Figgin over so that the sealed side is on the bottom. Cut slits into the center to vent. Place the Figgin, sealed side down, on a parchment-lined baking sheet.

7. Repeat steps 5–6 until you have 9 Figgins on the baking sheet.

8. Bake for 20 minutes, or until golden brown.

SPOO

SERVES 10

Babylon 5 is a space-opera series that ran for five years in the 1990s. The series features a good amount of strange alien foods, but the most intriguing (and perhaps the most disgusting) is Spoo. Spoo ("Oops" spelled backward) actually makes its first appearance before *Babylon 5*, in *She-Ra:Princess of Power*, where it is offered to Skeletor, who quickly rejects it saying that he hates Spoo, even though he doesn't know what it is.

Spoo is made from a type of worm of the same name that is treated with contempt by most of the galaxy due to its annoying habit of sighing all the time. It is considered by many aliens to be the tastiest food in the galaxy; however, it doesn't seem to appeal to human tastes. Or Skeletor's.

INGREDIENTS

1 cup (50 g) panko bread
   crumbs
¾ cup (175 ml) buttermilk
1 packet (¼ oz, or 7 g) flavorless
   gelatin
3 tablespoons cold water
½ cup (40 g) shredded
   Parmesan cheese
1 pound (454 g) ground turkey
1 egg, lightly beaten
6 cloves garlic, minced
2 tablespoons onion powder
½ tablespoon powdered
   chicken bouillon
Salt and pepper, to taste
Blue food coloring (optional)

1. In a large bowl, combine the panko and buttermilk, and set aside for about 10 minutes to form a panade (bread paste). In another bowl, combine the gelatin and water, stir, and set aside for 10 minutes to allow the gelatin to stiffen a bit.

2. Preheat the oven to 400°F (200°C).

3. Add the remaining ingredients to the panko and buttermilk in the large bowl and tip in the gelatin and its water. Mix everything together thoroughly.

4. Line a loaf tin with parchment paper and pour in the Spoo, smoothing the top.

5. Bake for 45 minutes, or until the center of the Spoo reaches at least 165°F (75°C). This is very important! There is poultry in this dish, which is dangerous to consume raw.

6. Remove the Spoo from the oven and leave to cool and set for about 10 minutes. There will probably be a brown layer on top that will be removed later for aesthetic reasons, and a good amount of juice will escape and look very gross, but, trust me, it will taste good.

7. Use a knife to cut the loaf into cubes, removing the browned top from each, and serve! I like to skewer my chunks onto little toothpicks.

CRAM

SERVES 5-6

I get a surprising amount of requests for Cram, the characteristically unexciting biscuit-like food from *The Lord of the Rings*, which is testament to the dedication for which Tolkien fans are renowned. Cram is so unexciting that in *The Hobbit*, Tolkien describes eating it as a "chewing exercise." Its few redeeming qualities are that it is so dry that it keeps indefinitely and that it provides adequate sustenance. This food is not to be confused with Cram from *Fallout*, which is a play on the canned mystery meat that is Spam.

This recipe is for a very dry cookie or biscuit that has protein powder added for sustenance and apple sauce for extra nutrients. Additional sugar and apple sauce (1 to 2 tablespoons) can be added to make the biscuit less dry and bland if you're more concerned with taste than you are with accuracy. Enjoy?

INGREDIENTS

¼ cup (60 ml) vegetable oil,
   plus extra for greasing
½ cup (40 g) ground instant oats
¼ cup (30 g) unflavored whey
   protein powder
¼ cup (30 g) flour
3 tablespoons sugar
Pinch salt
Pinch baking powder
1 egg
2 tablespoons apple sauce

1. Preheat the oven to 375°F (190°C). Grease a 9 × 9-inch (23 × 23 cm) baking pan or line it with parchment paper.

2. In a large bowl, stir together the oats, protein powder, flour, sugar, salt, and baking powder.

3. In a separate bowl, whisk together the egg, apple sauce, and vegetable oil.

4. Add the wet ingredients to the dry ingredients and stir thoroughly with a wooden spoon.

5. Add the mixture to the greased pan, making sure the batter settles evenly.

6. Bake for 12–15 minutes, or until the Cram is firm and a fork or toothpick inserted into it comes out clean. Cut into squares and serve!

FISH FINGERS AND CUSTARD

SERVES 4-6

INGREDIENTS

FISH FINGERS
½ cup (60 g) flour
Salt and pepper, to taste
2 eggs
1 tablespoon milk
1 cup (50 g) panko bread
   crumbs
1 cup (70 g) coconut flakes
1 pound (454 g) tilapia filets,
   cut into 1-inch (2.5 cm) strips
   (cod or haddock will
   also work)
Oil, for frying

"CUSTARD"
½ cup (115 g) mayonnaise
2 tablespoons yellow mustard
   (prepared)
1 tablespoon Dijon mustard
2 tablespoons honey
1 tablespoon lemon juice
2 cloves garlic, minced

Fish Fingers and Custard became a thing when the eleventh incarnation of the Doctor first regenerated outside the home of a young Amelia Pond. His regeneration made him very hungry but, having a whole new body, he had no idea what sort of food tasted good to his new taste buds. So, he enlisted the help of his new red-headed pal to help him find out what he liked. After rejecting a multitude of different foods, he found something that he liked. Yep, fish fingers dipped in custard.

Let's face it, the idea is meant to be sort of strange and unappealing. In the scene, Matt Smith himself is actually eating breaded coconut cakes dipped in custard. Since making the recipe, though, a lot of Whovians have told me that plain old store-bought fish fingers and regular vanilla custard actually taste pretty okay. I'll take their word for it and bless them all for their dedication . . . but I wanted to make something that everyone could get down with.

My recipe pairs a panko and coconut–battered fried fish finger (coconut added as tribute to the reality of the scene) and tangy lemon and honey mustard dipping sauce (that basically looks like custard) which complements it perfectly.

1.   **To make the fish fingers:** Combine the flour, salt, and pepper in a shallow bowl. Beat the eggs with the milk in another shallow bowl. Mix the bread crumbs and coconut in a third shallow bowl.

2.   Coat each fish strip in the seasoned flour, dip them into the egg mixture, and then roll in the panko and coconut mixture. Set aside until ready to cook.

3.   Heat ½ inch (13 mm) of oil in a large skillet over medium-high heat. In small batches, fry the fish sticks until golden brown, about 2 minutes per side. Drain on a paper towel–lined plate.

4.   **To make the "custard":** Simply combine all the ingredients and mix thoroughly.

5.   Liberally dip the fish fingers in the custard and enjoy!

ELSWEYR FONDUE

SERVES 4

INGREDIENTS

MOON SUGAR (OPTIONAL)
½ cup (120 ml) water
3 catnip tea bags
⅓ cup (80 ml) corn syrup
2 tablespoons mesquite flavor
2 teaspoons cayenne pepper,
  or to taste
1 tablespoon smoked paprika,
  or to taste
1 cup (200 g) granulated sugar
Confectioners' sugar,
  for coating

FONDUE
1 clove garlic
2 tablespoons butter
½ cup (120 ml) ale
8 ounces (225 g) crumbled
  blue cheese
¾ cup or 6 ounces (175 g)
  cream cheese
2 pieces Moon Sugar, optional
Bite-sized pieces of your
  favorite fruits, veggies,
  breads, and meats, for
  dipping

The Elder Scrolls is a video-game series that is chock-full of delicious-sounding made-up foods, and it was difficult to pin down just the right one to put in this collection. As I have a weakness for cheese, this one stood out. In the world of *Elder Scrolls*, Elsweyr is the home of the Khajiit race, which you may recognize as the big humanoid kitties. Elsweyr Fondue is made with three ingredients: Ale, Eidar cheese, and Moon Sugar. When eaten, it restores a massive amount of magicka.

So, Eidar cheese is very obviously a blue cheese, and ale is pretty self-explanatory, but the Moon Sugar is a bit of a question mark. Moon Sugar is an alchemy ingredient in the game that restores magicka, and is also used in the creation of Skooma, an illegal substance. It looks like brown crystals and is said to be made from a cane plant, like regular sugar. It is known to have a narcotic effect, especially on Khajiit, so that reminded me a little of catnip. Though we all love watching our cats act like furry little fools when exposed to the substance, catnip is not something that humans often consume, except, occasionally, as a mildly tranquilizing tea. So, I made a catnip tea-infused hard candy (for a crystalized look) and added some mesquite flavor. Admittedly, the Moon Sugar tastes pretty strange by itself but adds a nice smoky sweetness to the fondue. You will definitely have more Moon Sugar than you need for the fondue (the nature of hard candy makes it impossible to make it in small batches), so alternatively, if you don't want to end up with a bunch of extra Moon Sugar, you can skip making it all together and just add a pinch of mesquite and regular sugar to the fondue.

Enjoy the fondue with an assortment of veggies, fruits, bread, and meats. Hot tip: It goes especially well with steamed broccoli, apples, crusty bread, and tangy/spicy meats. Sugar and sand, furlicker!

1. **To make the moon sugar (optional):** Boil the water and brew the 3 tea bags for 0–15 minutes, until a strong concentrate is made. Remove the tea bags, squeezing out any excess liquid, and discard. Pour the brewed catnip tea into a good-quality metal saucepan with a candy thermometer attached, along with the corn syrup, spices, and granulated sugar.

2. Heat the mixture until it reaches 300°F (150°C), stirring constantly. Transfer the mixture to a heat-resistant container lined with parchment paper and sprinkle the confectioners' sugar over the top. Let the candy cool and harden.

3. When the candy is hard, use a butter knife to break it into pieces roughly the size of Jolly Ranchers. Coat with more confectioners' sugar if desired. The end product should look a bit like sea glass. You will have much more than needed for the Fondue, so you can either discard the excess or crush it up and use it as a rub for meat.

4. **To make the fondue:** Cut the garlic clove in half and rub the cut sides around the inside of a fondue pot. When done, leave the garlic in the pot. Add the butter to the pot and turn the heat on the fondue machine to 200°F (95°C). Let the butter melt for a few seconds.

5. Pour the ale into the pot. Begin to slowly add the crumbled blue cheese to the ale and stir in. When the cheese starts to melt, add the cream cheese and stir until the fondue is smooth.

6. If using moon sugar, add it to the pot and stir for about a minute more. The moon sugar will melt gradually and infuse the fondue with a sweet, smoky flavor, but it will not melt completely right away.

7. Dip the sides of your choice into the fondue and enjoy!

POPPLERS

SERVES 5-7

Popplers appeared in the season 2 episode "The Problem with Popplers," which is a play on the classic *Star Trek* episode "The Trouble with Tribbles." In the *Futurama* episode, the crew is running low on food supplies and goes to the nearest planet to see if they can find something edible. Lela stumbles upon a pit of edible creatures that turn out to be both delicious and addictive. They bring a large cargo of the irresistible snacks back to civilization, where they name them Popplers, and they quickly become a sensation. They look exactly like deep-fried shrimp and are eventually sold at Fishy Joe's restaurant.

INGREDIENTS

1 cup (240 g) buttermilk
2 eggs
1 pound (454 g) medium
  shrimp, cleaned, peeled, and
  tails removed
2 cups (250 g) flour, divided
1 cup (50 g) panko bread
  crumbs
1 tablespoon onion powder
1 tablespoon garlic powder
1 tablespoon Old Bay seasoning
Salt and pepper, to taste
Cayenne pepper, to taste
Canola oil, for deep-frying
Dipping sauces (optional)

1. In a small bowl, thoroughly whisk together the buttermilk and eggs. Add the shrimp to buttermilk-egg mixture and set aside.

2. In a medium bowl, mix together 1 cup (125 g) of the flour with the panko and seasonings. Put the remaining 1 cup (125 g) flour in a separate small shallow bowl.

3. Prepare a deep fryer—if you don't have one, fill a heavy-bottomed pot three-quarters full of canola oil. Heat the oil to 370°F (190°C). If you have a fry basket, set it into the deep fryer or pot full of oil. Make sure it is dry before doing so.

4. Remove the shrimp from the buttermilk bath and roll them in the plain flour until coated. Then, dunk them back into the buttermilk-egg bath, remove again, and roll in the panko-flour mix until coated. Repeat this step for every shrimp. This can be done in batches of 5 or 6 shrimp; you want to fry them in batches of this size because adding too many at once can cause safety issues and reduce the temperature of the oil, which will make the batter soggy.

5. Drop one batch of shrimp into the deep fryer at a time. Remove by carefully lifting the fry basket out of the deep fryer or pot after 1 or 2 minutes, or when the shrimp are golden and crispy. If you do not have a fry basket, use tongs to remove the shrimp. Be very careful not to get splashed with hot oil! Repeat until all Popplers are fried. Enjoy with a dipping sauce of your choice.

CHEESE BUNS

MAKES 20 BUNS

The Hunger Games seems to be really polarizing amongst nerds. There are some who seem to hate it and many more who love it. It might be because the story is often compared to (and even accused of copying) *Battle Royale*. Personally, having read and watched both of them, I think they are completely different stories. And, let's face it, pitting people (even children) against each other in a fight to the death is hardly a new concept. I don't think one is better than the other, but there is one way in which *The Hunger Games* excels over *Battle Royale*: food!

There are a lot of mouthwatering food moments in *The Hunger Games*. A lot. The moments are extra delicious as you experience them from the perspective of a character who has been malnourished most of her life. One of the more memorable foods is Katniss' favorite baked good from Peeta's bakery: the Cheese Bun. They are described as buns baked with a layer of cheese on top. Seriously, who doesn't like bread and cheese? Carb + melted cheese = heaven, amiright?

INGREDIENTS

3 cups (360 g) flour, divided
1 packet (¼ oz, or 7 g) active
   dry yeast
1 tablespoon sugar
1 teaspoon salt
¾ cup (88 g) shredded sharp
   cheddar cheese, divided
¾ cup (88g) shredded Gruyère
   cheese, divided
½ cup (120 ml) warm milk
½ cup (120 ml) warm water
1½ tablespoons olive oil
Butter, vegetable oil, or
   nonstick spray, for greasing
3 tablespoons butter, melted

1. Combine 1½ cups (180 g) of the flour, the sugar, salt, and yeast in a large bowl and thoroughly mix. Toss in ½ cup (58 g) of each cheese. Add the warm milk, warm water, and the olive oil, and beat for about 2 minutes.

2. Gradually stir in the remaining 1½ cups (180 g) flour until you have a soft dough. Tip out the dough onto a floured board and knead until it is elastic and not sticky, adding more flour if necessary. Place in a greased bowl and then flip the dough over to grease the other side. Cover the bowl with plastic wrap. Let the dough rise in a warm environment for about 30 minutes.

3. Punch the dough down, cover again, and let rest for 10 more minutes.

4. Cut the dough into 20 pieces and shape each one into a sphere. Dip each ball in melted butter and arrange the balls in two rows in the pan. Cover with a paper towel. Leave to rise in a warm place for about 1 hour, or until the balls have almost reached the top of the pan.

5. Preheat the oven to 375°F (190°C) and grease a small pan.

6. Sprinkle the remaining cheeses over the rolls.

7. Bake on the lower rack of the oven for 35 minutes, or until the rolls are firm and golden. They're done when you can insert a toothpick into the center of a bun and it comes out clean. Cool for 5 minutes, then enjoy.

LEMBAS

SERVES 10-15

Lembas is the quintessential geeky fictional food. It made its first appearance in Tolkien's *The Fellowship of the Ring*. The flavor of Lembas is never detailed but it is said to be able to fill the belly of a grown man in a few bites, which makes it useful for long journeys. It's also supposed to taste more pleasant than its non-elvish counterpart, Cram (page 19). If it were not for Lembas, Frodo and Sam would probably not have survived the extremely perilous journey through Mordor.

This is my second variation on Lembas. The nuts and the protein powder make it extremely filling; they will definitely make you feel like you just ate a big dinner. The citrus zest adds vitamins and the honey makes the bread both fragrant and tasty. They are soft, lightly sweet, and very delicate, so it's somewhat of a surprise when you start to feel like you just ate Thanksgiving dinner. I recently took some with me on a hiking excursion. I pretended I was climbing Mount Doom and kept calling my husband "Mr. Frodo." He didn't appreciate it, but the Lembas definitely kept my energy up.

INGREDIENTS

6 tablespoons olive oil, divided
1½ cups (350 ml) warm water
2½ cups (300 g) all-purpose flour
1 tablespoon instant yeast
1 cup (120 g) unflavored whey protein powder
2 cups (268 g) finely chopped macadamia nuts
1 tablespoon orange zest
¾ cup (255 g) honey
1 teaspoon salt
5 drops orange flower water (optional)
Large non-poisonous leaves (banana leaves recommended; optional)

1. Grease a 9 × 13-inch (23 × 33 cm) baking pan and add 3 tablespoons of the olive oil to the bottom.

2. Combine all the remaining ingredients, including the remaining 3 tablespoons olive oil, and beat at high speed with an electric mixer for one minute.

3. Transfer the batter to the prepared pan. Cover and let rise at room temperature for 1 hour.

4. While the dough is rising, preheat the oven to 375°F (190°C).

5. Bake the brsead until it is golden brown, 25–30 minutes. Remove from the oven, wait 5 minutes, and then turn it out of the pan onto a rack.

6. Cut the bread into square pieces, wrap each piece with a leaf, and tie with twine.

SOYLENT GREEN

SERVES 4

Soylent Green is a dystopian classic. It takes place on a future Earth where almost all of the world's resources have been depleted due to the sheer number of humans occupying the planet. Most of the overwhelming population survives, barely, on rations. Soylent Green is the newest of these rations. It is supposedly made from "high-energy plankton" and is much more nutritious than its predecessors, Soylent Red and Yellow.

Soylent Green appears in the movie as an unremarkable green-colored square. The taste is not described, though it is supposedly tastier than both Red and Yellow. Most people nowadays know the big "secret" of Soylent Green before they even watch the movie. Charlton Heston's dramatic acting at the film's climax is just too much fun to imitate. *SPOILER ALERT* I skipped the people (OMG, people!) and made a delicious cracker using furikake as the "high-energy plankton," cuz, you know, oceans. Turns out that people (and/or high-energy plankton) tastes pretty great dipped in hummus! I know, I know, everything tastes great dipped in hummus.

INGREDIENTS

2 cups (60 g) fresh spinach
1 egg
½ cup or 1 stick of butter
(120 g), at room temperature
¾ cup (60 g) shredded
Parmesan cheese
½ cup (50 g) high-energy
plankton (furikake)
Garlic powder, to taste
Onion powder, to taste
1½ cups (180 g) flour
Yellow food coloring (optional)
Green food coloring (optional)

1. Puree the spinach in a food processor.

2. In a large bowl, combine the pureed spinach, egg, butter, cheese, furikake, and garlic and onion powders. Mix thoroughly.

3. Add the flour and combine to form a dough. If desired, add a few drops of each food coloring into the dough and evenly work it in. Chill the dough in the refrigerator for 1 hour.

4. Preheat the oven to 400°F (200°C) and line a baking sheet with parchment paper.

5. Place a sheet of wax paper on top of a flat surface and, working in batches, place a handful of dough on the wax paper and then place another sheet of wax paper on top. Use a pastry roller or rolling pin to roll out the dough until it's about 1/8 inch (3 mm) thick.

6. Remove the top sheet of wax paper and use a square cookie cutter, about 3 × 3 inches (7.5 × 7.5 cm) in size, to shape the crackers, setting aside the excess dough to re-roll for the next batch.

7. Place the squares on the parchment-lined baking sheet, cover with aluminum foil to prevent browning, and bake for 15–20 minutes, or until crispy. You may need to bake them in batches.

8. Let cool before serving.

FRUITY OATY BARS

MAKES 12 BARS

Not that anything could ever make the cancellation of *Firefly* okay, but there was, in fact, a movie that dulled a minuscule portion of the grief and suffering. *Serenity* takes place a few months after where *Firefly* left off, and follows the crew of *Serenity* as they try to keep escaped experiment subject River Tam hidden from The Alliance.

In the film, there is a humorously bizarre commercial for a product called Fruity Oaty Bars that carries a subliminal signal to seek out River Tam. The bar itself seems to be rainbow colored (though that might just be the wrapper) and presumably tastes of fruit and oats. So, I made a super-tasty baked goody with oatmeal and dried fruits. Warning: Your mind will be blown and a live octopus might come out of your blouse. Also, keep out of reach of mice. Make a batch of these and pass them around your *Firefly* support group!

INGREDIENTS

2 cups (160 g) oats
1 cup (150 g) chopped nuts, of
  your choice
2 cups (300 g) dried fruit, of
  your choice
¼ cup (30 g) flour
Pinch ground cinnamon
Pinch allspice
½ cup or 1 stick (120 g) butter,
  melted
1 cup (240 ml) milk
1 egg
2 tablespoons brown sugar
1 teaspoon vanilla extract
Multiple food coloring colors
  (optional)

1. Preheat the oven to 350°F (180°C) and line a baking sheet with parchment paper.

2. In a large bowl, stir together the oats, nuts, dried fruit, flour, cinnamon, and allspice.

3. In another bowl, combine the butter, milk, egg, brown sugar, and vanilla extract, and thoroughly whisk together.

4. Add the wet ingredients to the bowl with the dry ingredients and mix together, making sure everything is evenly combined.

5. If you're going to dye the bars, evenly separate the mixture into as many different containers as you have colors. Add a few drops of the food coloring to each of the separated batters and mix until the colors are evenly dispersed.

6. Pour everything into the prepared baking sheet, making sure to flatten and even out the batter as much as possible. If you're using dyed batter, pour in one color at a time, starting from one side of the baking sheet and working toward the other, creating a rainbow effect.

7. Bake for 30-40 minutes, or until the top is crispy, but not burnt.

8. Let cool to room temperature, cut into rectangular bars, and serve!

PEANUT CHEESE BARS

MAKES 8 BARS

INGREDIENTS

5 graham crackers

1 tablespoon light brown sugar

$^2/_3$ cup (160 g) plus 1 tablespoon unsalted butter, melted, divided

2 cups (225 g) finely shredded cheddar cheese

2 cups (350 g) milk chocolate chips

1 cup (240 ml) half-and-half

½ cup (75 g) peanuts

Sprig parsley, for garnish (optional)

Earthbound is a fun and quirky old-school RPG, sort of a mix of a children's television show and a stoner's sci-fi dream fantasy. It also has a really interesting and complex food system, which makes it my kind of game. It was a little difficult to decide which food to include here because there are so many interesting options. For me, and I don't think I'm alone in this, the Peanut Cheese Bar has always stood out the most. Unfortunately (or fortunately, depending on your perspective), Trout Yogurt and Piggy Jelly didn't make the cut.

The Peanut Cheese Bar is the favorite food of the lovable species Mr. Saturn. Besides containing both peanuts and cheese, little is known about the bars other than that they are supposed to taste "pretty yummy" and recover 100 HP. If you're the kind of person who loves to combine salty and sweet, you will love this recipe. I didn't want to shy away from getting a real cheesy flavor, so I used sharp cheddar, but a milder cheese can be used instead. ZOOM!

1. Crush the graham crackers as thoroughly as possible. Add the brown sugar and ⅓ cup (80 g) of the melted butter to the crushed crackers and thoroughly combine all the ingredients.

2. Firmly press the graham-cracker mixture onto the bottom of a 6 × 6-inch (15 × 15 cm) container lined with parchment paper and place it in the fridge to set.

3. In a mixing bowl, combine the shredded cheese and ⅓ cup (80 g) of the melted butter until a paste-like texture is achieved.

4. Spread and lightly press this cheese paste on top of the set graham cracker layer to create the second layer, then return the container to the fridge.

5. Gently heat the half-and-half on the stove, stirring constantly.

6. Place the chocolate chips in a heatproof bowl and add the hot half-and-half while stirring. Let sit for a few minutes.

7. Add the remaining 1 tablespoon melted butter to the chocolate mixture and mix thoroughly until smooth.

8. Carefully and evenly spread the chocolate layer over the cheese layer. Evenly sprinkle the peanuts on top of the chocolate layer and gently press them in so they are partially submerged.

9. Return the container to the fridge for about 1 hour.

10. When ready to serve, cut into 8 rectangular pieces. Garnish with a sprig of parsley. Or don't...

PIZZA GYOZA

SERVES 3-5

Pizza has been an important part of *TMNT* from the very beginning. Any fan knows that the heroes in half shells, like most people with functioning taste buds, have a very passionate love for pizza. As an '80s baby, I grew up watching the original *TMNT* TV series. My personal favorite episode revolved around killer pizza monsters that hatched out of mutant meatballs, which Shredder planted on April O'Neil's pizza. It was totally tubular, dudes.

Since then, the turtles have had quite a few makeovers. Pizza Gyoza made its first appearance in the 2012 episode "Never Say Xever," when the turtles rescue Mr. Murakami, the blind owner of a local noodle house, from the Purple Dragons. In thanks, Murakami-san asks if he can prepare them a meal based on their favorite food. This seemingly unholy union is a bodacious fusion of pizza, the ubiquitous favorite food of the American teen, and traditional Japanese pot stickers, the snack of choice in Japan. Watch out, they're eye-poppingly tasty. *Booyakasha!* Or *Cowabunga!* if you were born before 1995.

½ cup (110 g) tomato sauce
1 tablespoon grated Parmesan
1 teaspoon dried oregano
5-6 fresh basil leaves,
  chiffonade
Savory Seasoning Blend
  (page 12), to taste
20 (about ½ package) gyoza
  wrappers, thawed
10 ounces (300 g) mozzarella
  cheese, shredded
10 ounces (300 g) pepperoni,
  chopped small
2 cloves garlic, roasted and
  minced
2 tablespoons vegetable oil,
  for frying
Marinara sauce, for dipping

1. In a small bowl, mix together the tomato sauce, Parmesan, oregano, basil, and seasoning. You can also add any other Italian seasonings you like to the sauce.

2. Prep your gyoza station. You will need a clean surface, preferably wood as the dough is less apt to stick to it. Have a small bowl of water, clean towel, and a baking sheet lined with parchment paper at the ready.

3. Take one gyoza wrapper and lay it on the clean surface. Spread about 1 teaspoon of the tomato sauce in the center of the gyoza, leaving plenty of room in the outside of the circle. The sauce should only take up about half the diameter of the gyoza skin.

4. Take a pinch of mozzarella cheese and sprinkle on top of the pizza sauce. Do the same with the chopped pepperoni.

5. Wet your fingers in the water and lightly moisten the edges of the gyoza wrapper, then dry your fingers on the towel. Fold the dumpling over and press the moistened inner edges together to form a semicircle. Some people may want to get fancy and do pleats, but it's not necessary. Place the sealed dumpling on the prepared baking sheet.

6. Repeat steps 3-5 until all the gyoza skins are gone.

7. Heat some oil in a skillet over medium-high heat. Fry the gyoza, filling sides down, until the bottoms are nice and browned but not burnt—usually just a few minutes.

8. Reduce the heat to medium-low and add about ½ cup (120 ml) of water to the pan. Immediately cover with a lid to steam for 10-15 minutes.

9. Serve with chopsticks and a little bowl of marinara sauce for dipping.

SPECIAL BELL PEPPERS AND BEEF

SERVES 2-4

INGREDIENTS

1-2 tablespoons cooking oil, for frying

8 ounce (227 g) flank steak, thinly sliced (optional)

3 cloves garlic, minced

1½ cups (150 g) shiitake mushrooms, cleaned and sliced

2 green bell peppers, seeded and cut into long, thin slices

3 tablespoons low-sodium soy sauce

2 tablespoons rice vinegar

2 teaspoons grated peeled fresh ginger

Red chili oil, to taste

2 green onions, diagonally sliced

Sesame seeds, for topping

As the first anime to be broadcast on Cartoon Network's Adult Swim, *Cowboy Bebop* was, for many in the West, the gateway drug into adult anime. Everything—from the music, to the action, to the characters—was stylish and cool. This series inspired my friends and me to make some of our first (incredibly bad) attempts at cosplay. It involved BB guns and rolled-up printer paper "cigarettes." Fortunately, no yellow shorts.

As far as food, it's not all self-heating ramen and Ganymede Sea Rats. Very early in the first episode of the series, Jet tells Spike he is preparing "special" beef and bell peppers. Unfortunately, it turns out that they don't actually have the funds for beef, so the meal is really just stir-fried green bell peppers and what looks like mushrooms, and probably not the kind that make you see talking frogs. Spike has . . . an emotional moment. If you've collected some good bounties lately, you can easily upgrade this dish by adding some sliced flank steak. See you, Space Cowboy . . .

1. Heat the cooking oil in a large nonstick skillet over medium-high heat.

2. If you're using the steak, add it to the skillet and cook for 2-3 minutes, searing on one side. If you're not using steak, proceed to step 3.

3. Add the garlic, mushrooms, and bell peppers to the skillet, and cook for 2-3 minutes, stirring constantly. Remove the vegetables and beef (if using) from the pan.

4. Add the soy sauce, vinegar, ginger, and chili oil to the same pan and bring to a boil for 1 minute, or until the sauce thickens slightly.

5. Add back the vegetables and beef (if using) to the hot pan, along with the scallions. Toss everything to coat in the sauce, then sprinkle with the sesame seeds and serve.

WHITE DRAGON NOODLES

SERVES ABOUT 4

Blade Runner is a 1982 science-fiction film starring Harrison Ford as Rick Deckard, a man whose job as blade runner is to seek out rogue replicants (androids) and eliminate them. The film was based on a novel with my favorite title of all time: *Do Androids Dream of Electric Sheep?* by Phillip K. Dick. It's nice (for me, anyway) when food is central to introducing the protagonist of a story, especially when the scene is so memorable.

When you first see Deckard, he is waiting for a seat at the White Dragon noodle bar and is shortly called over to take a seat. He orders four of something on the menu, but the chef, speaking Japanese, insists that he only needs two. Deckard gives up on getting four, but adds that he also wants noodles. Visually, the noodles are nondescript, but Deckard seems to thoroughly enjoy them. As soon as he begins to eat, he is arrested. Apparently determined to finish his meal, Deckard continues to eat his noodles in the police car. Eating noodles in the back seat of a flying police car while Edward James Olmos drives may be a dream for some of us, but for Deckard it's an ominous beginning.

INGREDIENTS

8 ounces (227 g) dried soba
   noodles or spaghetti
1½ teaspoon garlic, minced
1 tablespoon mirin
1 tablespoon sake
1 teaspoon dashi powder
3 tablespoons soy sauce
1 teaspoon sesame oil
1 tablespoon rice vinegar
2 tablespoons vegetable oil
White sesame seeds,
   for topping
Chopped green onions,
   for topping

1. Cook the noodles per package directions. Drain them when they are finished cooking and set aside.

2. In a small bowl, combine all the ingredients—except the noodles, the vegetable oil, and the toppings. Taste and adjust the flavors as necessary.

3. In a large pan or wok, heat the vegetable oil over medium-high heat until it is hot enough to sizzle. Add the cooked noodles, followed shortly by the sauce. Cook for 3–5 minutes, stirring the noodles to make sure they are absorbing the sauce.

4. Serve in a bowl topped with the sesame seeds and chopped green onions.

EZTLITL STUFFED MUSHROOMS

SERVES 6-8

Although *World of Warcraft* has been a long-standing champ of the MMO genre, *Guild Wars 2*, with its beautiful graphics and emphasis on exploration, has given the MMO giant a run for its money. This game has really pushed the boundaries of what an MMO can be. The tough part about doing any MMO recipe is just picking which food to do. Especially when it comes to *Guild Wars 2*, which, as players know, has an array of mouthwatering consumables.

So, why Eztlitl Stuffed Mushrooms? Well—full disclosure—I needed more appetizer recipes. But also, don't they sound tasty? And who doesn't love stuffed mushrooms? Always a crowd-pleaser. In the game, these contain mushrooms (obviously), Eztlitl stuffing (bread, thyme, rosemary, shallot), and cheese. There's really not a lot of additional ingredients needed to make this combination amazing in real life. Enjoy!

INGREDIENTS

28 large white mushrooms
⅔ cup (160 ml) extra-virgin olive oil, divided
1 shallot, minced
2 garlic cloves, peeled and minced
Salt and black pepper, to taste
1 cup (50 g) fresh bread crumbs
½ cup (50 g) grated Parmesan/Romano blend, plus more for topping
1 tablespoon chopped fresh thyme
½ tablespoon chopped fresh rosemary
1 tablespoon Savory Seasoning Blend (page 12)

1. Preheat the oven to 400°F (200°C).

2. Stem the mushrooms and set the caps aside. Chop the stems very small, almost so they're minced.

3. Heat 2 tablespoons (30 ml) of the olive oil in a pan, add the shallot, garlic, and chopped stems. Season with salt and pepper. Sauté over medium heat for 15 minutes, or until the stems are browned and juicy. Be careful not to burn the garlic.

4. Stir the chopped stems and garlic with the bread crumbs, cheese, thyme, rosemary, and 2 more tablespoons (30 ml) of the olive oil in a medium bowl to blend. Stir in the seasonings.

5. Grease the baking sheet with about 1 tablespoon (15 ml) of the olive oil, to evenly coat.

6. Spoon the filling into the mushroom caps and arrange them on the baking sheet, filling side up.

7. Drizzle the remaining olive oil over the filling of each mushroom, then top with the extra cheese—make them as cheesy as you like!

8. Bake until the mushrooms are tender and the filling is heated through and golden on top, about 30 minutes. Serve hot!

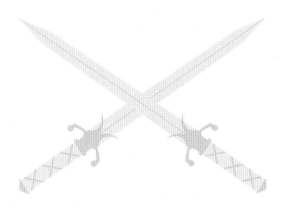

OTIK'S SPICED POTATOES

SERVES 2-4

Dragonlance began as a gaming module for *Dungeons and Dragons*, created by Tracy and Laura Hickman. It was submitted to TSR, the publishers of *Dungeons and Dragons*, and was well received because it was heavily focused on dragons, and the gaming modules at the time were perhaps a little more *Dungeons than Dragons*. Many series of novels have been created based on the module. There was even an animated movie based on the first book, but, despite its impressive cast, we do not speak of it.

The first trilogy, the *Dragonlance Chronicles* series, by Tracy Hickman and Margaret Weis, is beloved. In the *Dragonlance Chronicles* series there is an inn called the Inn of the Last Home, run by a portly man named Otik. Otik's specialty dish is spiced potatoes, which are famous far and wide. It's never specifically mentioned what the potatoes are spiced with, only that they are spiced and fried. Works for me! Enjoy with a nice pint of ale.

INGREDIENTS

½ cup or 1 stick (120 g) unsalted butter
1 dried red chili pepper
1 pound (454 g) fingerling potatoes, cut in half lengthwise
1 tablespoon Savory Seasoning Blend (page 12)
1 teaspoon paprika
½ teaspoon turmeric
½ teaspoon ground cumin

1. In a large skillet with a lid, heat the butter until it starts to bubble. Add the dried chili and move it around the pan, then let it infuse for about a minute.

2. Add the potatoes, then sprinkle on all the spices. Use a wooden spoon or a spatula to toss the potatoes around and make sure they are well coated in the butter and spices. At this point, remove the red chili. Cook on high heat for about 5 minutes, or until the potatoes are slightly browned at the edges.

3. Reduce the heat. Cook, covered, until the potatoes are fork tender.

4. Uncover the pan and increase the heat to evaporate any remaining moisture. The potatoes should be crispy on the outside and soft on the inside.

5. Taste and adjust the seasoning, if desired. Serve hot!

TASTEE WHEAT

SERVES 1–3

The Matrix had a huge cultural impact, setting all new standards for visual effects and action choreography and generating one of the biggest film followings since the first *Star Wars* trilogy. For a good stretch of the late '90s and early 2000s, it popularized sunglasses, black trench coats, and obnoxiously overused references. Really, the references never went away, just kinda dwindled slightly. Food is certainly not featured prominently in *The Matrix* trilogy, but what if I told you . . . Sorry, I had to.

It's not the most appetizing fictional food ever, but there is a fictional food in *The Matrix*—Tastee Wheat. While Neo and the rest of the crew are eating their gruel, aka. "bowls of snot," Mouse comments that the gruel reminds him of "Tastee Wheat" from inside the Matrix, and that everything may or may not taste like chicken because their only context is an illusionary world. It's not specified exactly what Tastee Wheat is, but one can surmise that it's a sort of hot wheat cereal. While you're eating this surprisingly satisfying porridge, you should try to remember that there is no spoon . . .

INGREDIENTS

2 cups (475 ml) water
Pinch salt
½ cup (100 g) bulgur
1 tablespoon whole wheat flour
½ cup (120 ml) whole milk
1 teaspoon Sweet Spice Blend
  (page 12)
1 teaspoon vanilla extract
Brown sugar, for topping
  (optional)
Butter, for topping (optional)

1. Pour the water into a pot, season with salt, and bring to a boil. Once boiling, stir in the bulgur, then cover and cook on low heat for 15 minutes.

2. Meanwhile, combine the flour, milk, spices, and vanilla extract in a small bowl, then add to the pot with the bulgur. Simmer until thickened. Add a little water if it becomes too thick.

3. Serve hot with brown sugar and butter (if using), or anything you'd normally put in oatmeal.

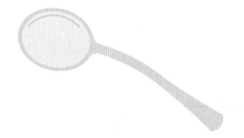

SOUPS
— AND —
STEWS

LAMB STEW WITH PLUMS

SERVES 5-6

INGREDIENTS

4-6 tablespoons olive oil, divided

3 pounds (1.4 kg) bone-in lamb

2 onions, chopped

5 cloves garlic, sliced

6 carrots, roughly chopped

6 ribs celery, roughly chopped

1½ cups whole dried plums

28-ounce (794 g) can whole peeled tomatoes, halved

1 cup (240 ml) dry white wine

1 cup (240 ml) beef stock

1 tablespoon fresh chopped thyme

2 tablespoons ground cumin

2 tablespoons paprika

Salt and pepper, to taste

Cayenne pepper, to taste

Cooked wild rice, for serving (optional)

Pistachio nuts, for garnish (optional)

This is heroine Katniss Everdeen's favorite food from The Capitol and it is an absolutely essential geeky food. In the first book, Katniss describes this stew as "incredible" and even tells Hunger Games host Caesar Flickman that it's what she finds most impressive in The Capitol. I'm with you 100 percent, Katniss. Food FTW. Later in the book, when Katniss and Peeta are slowly starving in a cave, Haymitch sends them a parcel of the stew. The specific flavors of the stew are not described. All that is known is that it contains lamb and dried plums and is sometimes served over wild rice, a combination that Katniss finds "perfect." Not to toot my own horn (toot! toot!), but my version is absolutely delicious and is the perfect meal after a long day of terror and fighting for your life.

1. Heat 2-3 tablespoons of the olive oil in a large pan over a high heat and sear the lamb until it gets a good color and doesn't burn. Remove the lamb from the pan and set aside.

2. Sauté the onions and garlic in the remaining 2-3 tablespoons olive oil in the same pan over a medium-high heat until the onions become translucent and soft. Then add the chopped carrots and celery, and sauté for another 7 minutes, or until the vegetables begin to soften.

3. Add the remaining ingredients—except the pistachios and wild rice—to a soup pot or Dutch oven, along with the lamb and sautéed vegetables, and stir together, making sure everything is evenly incorporated.

4. Simmer over a low heat for at least 2 hours, or until the lamb is tender and falling off the bone. You will need to periodically check on it, stir, taste, and adjust the spices, if necessary.

5. When done, remove the bones from the stew and discard. Break up the pieces of lamb with a spoon.

6. Serve over a bed of cooked wild rice (if using) and top with the pistachios (if using).

BOWL O' BROWN

SERVES 5-6

There are many, many mouthwatering descriptions of food in George R. R. Martin's epic tale, and one might wonder why I chose the questionable back-alley concoction of King's Landing's poorest folk (that phrase works two ways!) to put in this collection. I'm not sure why, but I think most would agree that it's one of the more memorable dishes in the series. It might be the mystery of what's inside, which frequently includes rats, pigeons, and possibly, in some of the more dubious pot shops, a very unfortunate person. Of course, there are also turnips, barley, carrots, and other humble vegetables. Arya Stark was prone to wolfing down (pun not intended, but I'm happy with it) a nice Bowl o' Brown during her time as a street urchin in King's Landing.

This recipe is definitely flexible; pretty much anything can be added to it. I recommend choosing at least three different kinds of cheap meat that you're not entirely comfortable with, because what's an *ASoIaF/Game of Thrones* recipe without a little discomfort? I used chicken legs, pork chump end, and oxtail, and it turned out pretty fantastic. Of course, no meat is turned down, so if that one person that drives you up the wall were to suddenly disappear . . . *

*Don't kill people; leave the assassination to Arya.

INGREDIENTS

2 pounds (907 g) meat(s)
of your choice (preferably
cheaper cuts with bones)
Salt and pepper, to taste
6 tablespoons butter, divided
1½ large yellow onions, peeled
and chopped
6 cloves garlic, chopped
6 medium mushrooms, sliced
2 turnips, peeled and chopped
1 large potato, peeled and
chopped
2 medium carrots, chopped
32 ounces or 1 quart (1 L) beef
broth
16 ounces or 2 cups (475 ml) ale
¼ cup (60 ml) Worcestershire
sauce
½ cup (100 g) uncooked pearl
barley
1 bay leaf
Seasonings of your choice, to
taste (optional)
2 tablespoons flour

1. Season the meat with salt and pepper and brown in 3 tablespoons of the butter in a large pan. Add the browned meat to a slow cooker.

2. In the same pan in which you browned the meat, add the remaining 3 tablespoons butter, onions, and garlic, and sauté until the onions start to soften and turn translucent. Add the mushrooms and continue to sauté for a couple minutes. Finally, add the turnips, potato, and carrots, and sauté for 5 minutes.

3. Add the sautéed veggies to the slow cooker, then add the beef broth, ale, Worcestershire sauce, barley, bay leaf, salt and pepper, and any other seasonings you may want to use.

4. Cook in the slow cooker for at least 4 hours on a high heat setting.

5. Sprinkle a bit of flour into the soup and stir in—this will help thicken it—gradually adding more until you get the desired thickness.

6. Reduce the heat to low and cook for a couple more hours, or until the meat is tender. It gets better the longer it stews!

YETO'S SUPERB SOUP

SERVES 8–10

As mentioned in the introduction, this was the recipe that inspired me to create *Geeky Chef*, so it holds a very dear place in my heart and stomach.

In *Twilight Princess*, Link is told that a monster has been seen around Zora's domain and seems to have an affinity for reekfish, which is a sort of red-colored fish known for its pungent smell. Upon finding the "monster," you discover that he is a yeti named Yeto who lives in the Snowpeak Ruins with his wife. The Yeti's wife (Yeta) has fallen ill and the reekfish is needed to go in the soup that will make her feel better. Yeto prepares the soup's reekfish base, but he wants to add more ingredients to make the soup even better. So, he sends you off to retrieve a pumpkin and some goat cheese from a different area of the ruins. There's just something about coming back to the warm kitchen of the icy abandoned ruins where Yeto is brewing a giant cauldron of soup that's very comforting.

This recipe is pretty simple because I wanted the three main ingredients to shine. This is truly one of my favorite soups, and I hope you guys enjoy it as much as I do!

INGREDIENTS

2 pounds (907 g) kabocha or pumpkin, seeded, peeled, and diced
1 medium white onion, chopped
5 cloves garlic, cut into quarters
¼ cup (50 ml) olive oil
4½ cups (1 L) fish, chicken, or vegetable stock, divided
1–2 salmon fillets
Salt and pepper, to taste
½ cup (75 g) goat cheese
About 1 cup (240 ml) cream
Fresh basil leaves, to taste

1. Preheat the oven to 375°F (190°C).

2. Toss the pumpkin, onion, and garlic in a large bowl with the olive oil until they are all coated.

3. Roast the vegetables in the oven on a baking sheet until they are tender, about 45 minutes, and have nice browned edges. Transfer to a soup pot over medium heat.

4. Add 3¾ cups (880 ml) of the stock to the pot and simmer for up to 45 minutes, or until all the vegetables are fully cooked.

5. Meanwhile, season the salmon fillets with a little salt and pepper and pan-fry until cooked through. Set aside.

6. Transfer the soup to a blender or food processor and blend until smooth (be careful with hot liquids)—you may need to do this in batches depending on the size of your blender or food processor.

7. Blend in small amounts of the goat cheese along with the cream. Add the remaining ¾ cup (180 ml) stock to the soup until it reaches the desired consistency.

8. Flake the cooked salmon and add to the soup.

9. Tear in a few basil leaves, taste the soup for flavor, and season with salt and pepper if needed.

ELIXIR SOUP

SERVES 5-7

You can probably see that I like *Zelda* a lot, as it has inspired many of the recipes in this book. So far, Elixir Soup has only appeared in one *Zelda* game, *The Windwaker*. *The Windwaker* is a bit of an underdog in the series because it is stylistically simple in comparison to the critically acclaimed and much-beloved *Ocarina of Time*.

Link receives this soup from his adorable grandmother after healing her illness with a captured fairy. The soup is bright yellow and is described as both healthy and hearty—it fully replenishes Link's life and magic bar and doubles his attack power! I can see why it's his favorite. And unlike other potions in the game, Link smiles when he drinks this.

INGREDIENTS

6 tablespoons butter
1 yellow onion, chopped
3 cloves garlic, minced
1 pound (454 g) yellow squash, chopped
2 carrots, chopped
¼ cup (40 g) chopped cauliflower
2 turnips, peeled and chopped
¼ cup (60 ml) lemon juice
1 yellow chili, seeded and chopped (optional)
32 ounces or 1 quart (1 L) chicken or veggie stock, divided
Salt and pepper, to taste
Yellow food coloring (optional)
Chives or green onions, finely chopped

1. Melt the butter in a large pot over medium-low heat and cook the yellow onion and garlic until softened, 8–10 minutes.

2. Add the squash, carrots, cauliflower, turnips, lemon juice, chili (if using), and half of the stock to the pot, and bring to a boil. Reduce the heat and simmer until the vegetables are very tender, about 20 minutes.

3. Remove from the heat and let cool for about 10 minutes, or until the soup won't burn you.

4. Transfer the soup to a blender or food processor and blend until smooth (be careful with hot liquids)—you may need to do this in batches depending on the size of your blender or food processor. Return to a saucepan or pot and season with the salt and pepper.

5. Simmer over low heat until ready to serve, adding more stock until the soup reaches the desired consistency. Add a few drops of the food coloring (if using).

6. Transfer the soup to your serving vessel (preferably a corked glass bottle) and sprinkle the chopped chives or green onions on the surface of the soup to garnish. Drink it with a smile!

PUMM'S HOT PUMPKIN SOUP

SERVES 2-4

I may have gone a tad overboard with the *Zelda* recipes in this cookbook. The heart wants what the heart wants. Not to mention, it's one of the most beloved video game series of all time.

This one appeared in *Skyward Sword*. In Pumpkin Landing, one of the sky islands surrounding Skyloft, there is a pub called The Lumpy Pumpkin. There, Link can buy some pumpkin soup from the pub owner, Pumm. Try saying that three times fast. . . . Although this is another pumpkin soup from *Zelda*, I wanted to make this one its own thing and have a different flavor profile. This recipe is for a warm, comforting, puréed pumpkin soup that's so delicious, you won't even care about all those pots and that really expensive chandelier that Link just broke.

INGREDIENTS

2 sugar pumpkins or 2½ cups (560 g) canned pure pumpkin, plus 1 sugar pumpkin, for serving
2 tablespoons olive oil, plus extra for brushing
5 shallots, peeled and diced
5 cloves garlic, minced
2 cups (475 ml) chicken or vegetable broth
1 cup (240 ml) coconut milk
2 tablespoons pure maple syrup
½ teaspoon allspice
½ teaspoon turmeric
½ teaspoon ground ginger
½ teaspoon thyme
Salt and black pepper, to taste
Savory Seasoning Blend (page 12), to taste
Toasted pepitas, to garnish

1. Preheat the oven to 350°F (180°C) and line a baking sheet with parchment paper. If using canned pumpkin, proceed straight to step 4.

2. Using a sharp knife, cut off the tops of the sugar pumpkins then halve both the vegetables. Use a sharp spoon to scrape out all of the seeds and strings.

3. Brush the flesh with oil and place the pumpkins face down on the baking sheet. Bake for 45–50 minutes, or until a fork easily pierces the skin. Remove from the oven and let cool for 10 minutes, then peel away the skin and set the pumpkins aside.

4. In a large saucepan, add the 2 tablespoons of olive oil, shallots, and garlic. Sauté over medium heat for about 5 minutes, or until slightly browned and translucent.

5. Add all the remaining ingredients and bring to a simmer.

6. Transfer the soup mixture to a blender and purée the soup, then pour the puréed mixture back into the cooking pot.

7. Continue cooking over medium-low heat for about 10 minutes. Adjust the seasonings to your preference.

8. Serve in a bottle or in another sugar pumpkin cut in half with the guts removed, if you like.

PLOMEEK SOUP

SERVES 8-10

This is a dish that has appeared throughout most of the *Star Trek* series, dating all the way back to *TOS*. It is a traditional breakfast dish of the Vulcans, also called Plomeek Broth. In the original series, Christine Chapel serves the soup to Spock during his Pon Farr (sort of like a Vulcan mating season—Vulcans become a little psychotic during this time), and Spock throws the bowl at her. There were many references and appearances on the *Enterprise* as the soup seemed to be a favorite of T'Pol.

Vulcans (unlike us illogical humans) eat for practical purposes only, not for pleasure, so most of their food is considered pretty bland and boring by human standards. Vulcans are also vegan by nature so their food does not contain any animal products. Plomeek soup is no different in those regards; however, the soup can be spiced up a bit. On *DS9*, Bashir orders it with a "touch of basil," and on *Voyager*, Neelix makes a version that Tuvok finds to be "too spicy." The soup doesn't seem to have a standard color or consistency, as it appears to look different each time it is shown, making it logical to assume that the dish is flexible. I have made a vegan soup that is simple tasting and nutritious (though probably a little "spicy" by Vulcan standards), served with just a touch of basil. Eat this and you will definitely live long and (maybe) prosper.

INGREDIENTS

2 tablespoons olive oil
1 leek, chopped
4 tablespoons minced garlic
1 medium carrot, peeled and
  chopped
½ cup (38 g) lima beans
½ cup (75 g) chopped
  cauliflower florets
1 cup (150 g) peas
64 ounces or 2 quarts (2 L)
  vegetable stock
3 medium tomatoes, chopped
1 cup (175 g) corn kernels
Salt and pepper, to taste
2 tablespoons fresh parsley,
  chopped
5 basil leaves, sliced into strips
2 teaspoons lemon juice

1. Heat the olive oil in a large stock pot with a lid over medium heat. Add the leek and garlic, and cook until the leek begins to soften.

2. Add the carrots, lima beans, cauliflower, and peas, and cook for about 5 more minutes, stirring occasionally.

3. Increase the heat to high and add the stock. Bring to a simmer.

4. Once it's simmering, add the tomatoes and corn. Reduce the heat to low and cook, with the pot covered, until the vegetables are tender enough to pierce easily with a fork, about 30 minutes. Don't overcook.

5. Season with the salt and pepper.

6. Transfer the soup to a blender or food processor and blend until smooth (be careful with hot liquids)—you may need to do this in batches depending on the size of your blender or food processor.

7. Add the parsley, basil, and lemon juice right before serving.

DRAGONBREATH CHILI

SERVES 8-12

I had to include something from the still undefeated champion of MMORPGs, *World of Warcraft*. *WoW* is the MMO version of Blizzard's 1994 hit game *Warcraft*. At the peak of its popularity, the game had over ten million subscribers worldwide. I myself have spent a good deal of my life in Azeroth and I don't regret it. Though the game has a reputation for being addictive and isolating, *WoW* has been an important place for geeks everywhere to gather and build a diverse and vibrant community. Spend, like, ten minutes in Barrens chat and you'll see what I mean.

As players know, there are hundreds of food items in *World of Warcraft*. The reason I chose Dragonbreath Chili is because it has one of the most dramatic food effects in the game. Also, chili is a great food to eat while playing *WoW* because it's easy to reheat, it's versatile, it's nutritious, and your keyboard won't get all greasy—plus, it's easy to reheat. I know pizza tends to be the gaming food of choice, but I'm telling you, chili is where it's at. This recipe is a modified version of my favorite gaming chili, made so hot you'll be breathing fire. The secret ingredient is coffee, which I know sounds kinda weird, but it adds a great depth of flavor and, of course, caffeine. Before you do your dailies, prep the chili and let it roll while you quest—an hour or two later, you'll have some delicious fuel to get you through the grind. I speak from experience.

INGREDIENTS

1 yellow onion, finely chopped

Butter or oil, for frying

1–2 habanero chilies, seeded and finely chopped

1–2 jalapeños, seeded and finely chopped

1 poblano chili, seeded and chopped

1 red bell pepper, seeded and chopped

6 cloves garlic, minced

2½ pounds (1.1 kg) ground mystery meat (your choice)

¾ cup (180 ml) spicy V8 juice

½ cup (120 ml) strong brewed coffee

2 × 15.5-ounce (439 g) cans red kidney beans, drained

2 × 14.5-ounce (411 g) cans diced tomatoes

8-ounce (227 g) can tomato sauce

4 tablespoons chili powder

4 tablespoons ground cumin

2 tablespoons onion powder

1 tablespoon smoked paprika

Salt and pepper, to taste

1. In a large pan, sauté the onion in some butter or oil over a medium-high heat for about 2 minutes. Add the chilies and red pepper and sauté for another 2 minutes. Add the garlic and continue to cook until everything is lightly caramelized, about 5 minutes.

2. In a separate pan, brown the ground mystery meat. Try not to break it up too much while browning if you want bigger pieces of meat in the chili. After it's done browning, drain the excess fat, if necessary.

3. Add the meat to the onions and peppers, and mix together. Transfer to a stock pot or Dutch oven over high heat, add the remaining ingredients, combine everything, and cook for 5 minutes, or until it starts to bubble.

4. Reduce the heat to low and simmer the chili, uncovered, for around 2 hours. Stir and taste periodically to see if you want to add more spices. Chili tends to burn and harden on the base of the pot, so it's good to scrape the bottom with a wooden spoon occasionally.

5. Serve with your favorite chili fixin's.

ROOTLEAF SOUP

SERVES 6-8

INGREDIENTS

2 tablespoons olive oil or unsalted butter

1 large or 2 medium white onions, chopped

1 teaspoon salt, plus more to taste

2 ribs celery with leaves, chopped

4 leeks, white and light green parts, thinly sliced

1 teaspoon black pepper, plus more to taste

1 head Savoy cabbage, chopped

4 cloves garlic, minced

2 russet potatoes, peeled and chopped

6 cups (1.5 L) vegetable broth

2 fresh bay leaves

3 tablespoons chopped flat-leaf parsley

Savory Seasoning Blend (page 12), to taste

¼ cup (60 ml) lemon juice

This little gem flies by so quickly that it's almost unnoticeable. In *Episode V*, Luke meets Yoda for the first time on Dagobah, although Luke doesn't realize that the little green guy is the Jedi Master he is seeking. Honestly, for someone who's apparently very strong in the Force, Luke seems to be a few midi-chlorians short. After some mysterious chitchat, Yoda invites Luke back to his hut, where he is preparing some sort of soup or stew in a cauldron. Yoda calls the soup "rootleaf" as Luke gulps down a bowl of the stuff.

Yoda was stranded on Dagobah after being exiled from the Jedi Order and likely had to make do with very limited resources, so this recipe is appropriately simple. The word "rootleaf" implies something leafy that comes from the ground, so I have chosen some leafy sprouting vegetables and a root vegetable as the stars of this entirely plant-based soup. Enjoy it, you will!

1. In a soup pot with a lid, warm the olive oil or butter over medium-high heat. Once the oil is hot, add the onion and sprinkle with the 1 teaspoon of salt. Stir the onion until it begins to turn translucent, 3-4 minutes.

2. Add the celery and leeks to the onion and stir. Add the 1 teaspoon of black pepper and continue cooking for another 5-6 minutes, stirring once every minute.

3. Add the cabbage and garlic, and cook, stirring occasionally, until the cabbage begins to caramelize, about 10 minutes.

4. Stir in the potatoes, vegetable broth, bay leaves, and parsley. Bring the soup to a simmer and cook, partly covered, until the potatoes begin to fall apart, 45-50 minutes. Add water, if needed, to reach the desired consistency.

5. Season the soup with the seasoning blend and salt and pepper (or anything else you think might taste nice), and stir in the lemon juice just before serving.

SEAWEED NOODLES

SERVES 2-3

The Last Airbender pushed the envelope of storytelling in family entertainment, but Korra took it even further and went to very unexpected places. *Legend of Korra* takes place in Republic City, seventy years after the events of *The Last Airbender*, in a time when the four elemental societies are united.

In Republic City, there's a noodle house in the Little Water Tribe neighborhood. You may remember it as Mako's first date spot of choice and where he goes to eat his feelings later. Their specialty is seaweed noodles, which their advertisements claim are the best in the city. There's no clarification on what exactly seaweed noodles are, but one can surmise that they're noodles made with seaweed, and are most likely served in a savory broth. I tried to use a lot of ingredients that I thought the water tribe would use, but you may have to visit an Asian grocery store to obtain some of them.

INGREDIENTS

NOODLES

2 sheets nori
½ cup (120 ml) lukewarm water
4 spinach leaves
2 drops green food coloring
  (optional)
1⅔ cups (170 g) high-gluten
  flour, plus extra for dusting
Pinch salt

SOUP

2 cloves garlic, minced
2 teaspoons sesame oil
6 cups (1.4 L) water
3 teaspoons instant dashi
2 pieces kombu
3 dried shiitake mushrooms
½ cup (40 g) dried wakame
1 tablespoon fish sauce, or to
  taste
1 tablespoon soy sauce, or to
  taste

SUGGESTED TOPPINGS

Green onions
Bonito flakes
Sliced Japanese fish cakes
Furikake

1. **To make the noodles:** Tear the nori into small pieces and put in a bowl with the water. Let sit until the nori is basically dissolved into the water. Add this and the spinach leaves into a blender, then blend until uniform. If you want greener noodles, you can blend in the green dye at this point.

2. Add the flour and salt into a large bowl. Pour the seaweed/spinach water slowly, a little at a time, into the bowl with the flour, carefully stirring with a wooden spoon. It should start to form crumbles, which is what you want.

3. Get your hands into the bowl and form the mixture into a dough, then knead the dough until it's smooth and elastic, about 10 minutes. At this time, evaluate the dough's color to see if it's green enough for you, keeping in mind the noodles will lose some color when they cook. You can knead in more food dye if you want it a bit greener. If the dough becomes sticky, sprinkle over a little more flour.

4. Cover the dough with a wet cloth and let it rest for about 30 minutes. Transfer the dough to a floured work surface, then roll it into a rectangular shape until it's almost paper-thin.

5. Now we're essentially making a jelly roll with the dough. Take one of the edges and fold the dough in by about 2 inches (5 cm). Continue to do this until the dough is completely rolled up, spreading some more flour after each fold to prevent sticking.

6. Cut the folded dough lengthwise into long, thin strips with a sharp knife. Carefully unfold the noodle strips and shake off the extra flour. Lay the noodles out on a baking sheet lined with parchment paper and set aside.

7. **To make the soup:** In a pot, sauté the minced garlic in the sesame oil for about a minute over medium heat. Add the water, dashi, kombu, and dried mushrooms to the pot and bring to a boil. Once the mushrooms are soft, add the wakame, fish sauce, and soy sauce. You can add more of the sauces if you like things saltier. Remove the kombu, then add the noodles to the soup and let them boil for 2–4 minutes, or until they are tender and cooked through.

8. Serve the soup in deep bowls with the toppings of your choice.

BUTTONS IN A BLANKET

SERVES 4-6

I have been itching to do something from a *Final Fantasy* game. Each game in the series has elements of fantasy and sci-fi and generally revolve around a group of heroes tasked with saving the world. There are many things the series is known for: stunning graphics, epic battles, crazy hairstyles . . . but food? Not so much. Historically, the consumables in the series have, for the most part, been nondescript potions and elixirs. However, the series finally got their chocobos in a row (foodwise) and added a lot of tasty-sounding consumables to the MMO and the newest console game.

Buttons in a Blanket is used in the quest "Comfort Me with Mushrooms" and is given as a reward for completing the quests "Just Another Bug Hunt" and "Made to Order." I chose this recipe not only for its adorable name but also because it's very similar to a favorite family recipe of mine. In the game, it's described as "button mushrooms wrapped in parboiled cabbage and stewed in a savory soup." The image in the game shows two stuffed cabbage rolls floating in a red (likely tomato-based) broth.

INGREDIENTS

1 head green cabbage

FILLING

½ tablespoon extra-virgin
  olive oil
1 white onion, chopped
2 cloves garlic, minced
2 cups (200 g) button (white)
  mushrooms, chopped
1 cup (165 g) wild rice, cooked
1 tablespoon Savory Seasoning
  Blend (page 12), or to taste
Salt and black pepper, to taste
½ cup (120 ml) white wine

SOUP

1 tablespoon olive oil
2 cloves garlic, minced
3 cups (675 g) tomato sauce
2 tablespoons packed brown
  sugar
2 tablespoons lemon juice
2 tablespoons Worcestershire
  sauce
2 tablespoons Savory
  Seasoning Blend (page 12)
Salt and black pepper, to taste
1½ cups (350 ml) white wine

1. Bring a large pot of salted water to a boil. Add the whole cabbage head, reduce the heat to a simmer, and let the cabbage cook for 3–5 minutes until the leaves are soft but not falling apart. Drain and set aside to cool.

2. **To make the filling:** Heat the olive oil in a saucepan with a lid over medium heat. Add the onion and sauté until it begins to soften, then add the garlic and sauté for a few more minutes.

3. Add the mushrooms, rice, and seasonings. Cover and cook over medium heat for about 5 minutes. Add the wine and continue to cook until all the liquid has either evaporated or been absorbed. Remove the pan from the heat and set aside to cool to about room temperature or a little higher.

4. Place the cooled filling in a food processor and process until fine. You can also use a knife, but it will take longer. Set aside.

5. **To make the soup:** Heat the olive oil in a saucepan over medium heat. Add the garlic and cook for 30 seconds. Add all the other ingredients—except the wine—and stir. Reduce the heat to low, then add the wine. Let simmer so the mixture begins to thicken, about 10 minutes.

6. Carefully peel the leaves from the cooled cabbage. You'll only want to use the largest, strongest leaves to make the rolls; the others you can just add to the soup unstuffed, if you like.

7. To assemble the rolls, lay one cabbage leaf on a flat surface. Place 1–2 tablespoons of filling (how much depends on the size of the leaf) in the center of the leaf. Fold in the sides, and roll up tightly, like a burrito, tucking in the ends. Repeat with the remaining leaves and filling.

8. Pour one-third of the tomato soup in the bottom of a saucepan or Dutch oven. Place each roll, seam side down, in the soup. Evenly pour the rest of the soup over the tops of the rolls. Cover and let the rolls simmer for 10–20 minutes, or until heated through.

9. To serve, place 2 rolls in a bowl and pour in the soup so it covers the rolls halfway.

CALAMARI GUMBO

SERVES 8-10

Bioware's *Mass Effect* is one of those games that changes everything. The series follows Commander Shepard and his/her crew as they fight to save the galaxy from the threat of the Reapers, a machine-race bent on destroying the galaxy. To people who haven't played the game, this summarization may seem like your basic sci-fi plot, but *Mass Effect* is anything but basic. It's full of innovative sci-fi goodness, with amazing visuals and superb characters. It's so well developed that it has inspired numerous spin-offs in multiple media, including novels, comics, and film.

This dish was also mentioned in *Mass Effect 2*, after Shepard retrieves some provisions for the Normandy's cook, Mess Sergeant Gardner. Sgt. Gardner will thank Shepard for providing better food and ask if you want to try his Calamari Gumbo, a recipe he learned from the Asari. Gardner questions why the Asari would have such a recipe, noting it's a bit cannibalistic, but admits the Asari know what they're doing when it comes to cuisine. If you choose to taste the gumbo, you are rewarded with an uncomfortable silence. Yay?

INGREDIENTS

CALAMARI

1 tablespoon olive oil
1 pound (454 g) squid, cleaned,
   bodies cut into ¾-inch
   (2 cm) thick rings, tentacles
   left whole, and patted dry
   with a paper towel
2 tablespoons unsalted butter
2 cloves garlic, minced
1 tablespoon Italian parsley
Salt and black pepper, to taste

SOUP

½ pound (227 g) Andouille
   sausage, sliced into thin discs
1 large yellow onion, finely diced
1 red bell pepper, finely diced
2 ribs celery, finely chopped
2 carrots, peeled and finely diced
5 cloves garlic, minced
½ cup or 1 stick (120 g)
   unsalted butter
½ cup (120 g) all-purpose flour
7 cups (1.7 L) fish stock
Salt and black pepper, to taste
Savory Seasoning Blend (page
   12), to taste
Cajun seasoning, to taste
½ pound (225 g) okra, sliced
   into thin discs
Cilantro or Italian parsley,
   for garnish
Chopped chives, for garnish

1. **To make the calamari:** In a large skillet, heat the olive oil over high heat until sizzling and just starting to smoke. Carefully add the squid to the pan, making sure the pieces are not touching or piling on top of each other. Add the butter, garlic, and parsley. Season with the salt and pepper.

2. Cook, tossing frequently, until the squid is no longer translucent and is cooked all the way through, about a minute or two. Be careful not to overcook the squid. Remove from the heat and set aside.

3. **To make the soup:** Heat a medium skillet over high heat. Add the andouille sausage and cook until browned on both sides. Set the sausage aside but don't drain the skillet.

4. In the same skillet, cook the onions, bell pepper, celery, carrots, and garlic until soft. Remove from the heat and set aside.

5. Create the roux. In a Dutch oven, melt the butter over medium heat. Gradually sprinkle in the flour, stirring occasionally. Cook the roux until it's a light-caramel color, 6 or 7 minutes.

6. Add the sautéed vegetables from step 4 to the roux and cook for a few more minutes.

7. In a large saucepan, bring the fish stock to a boil. Once the stock is hot, whisk about 6 cups (1.4 L) of the stock into the roux.

8. In the Dutch oven, bring the soup to a boil, then reduce the heat to a simmer. Add the sausage and okra and continue to simmer for about 20 minutes, adding calamari for the last couple minutes. You may need to add more stock if the mixture is too thick.

9. Season the soup to taste. Serve with cilantro, parsley, and chives.

WIFE SOUP

SERVES 8-10

INGREDIENTS

2 tablespoons olive oil or
  unsalted butter
1 large or 2 medium white
  onions, chopped
1 teaspoon salt, plus more to
  taste
2 ribs celery with leaves,
  chopped
2 cloves garlic, minced
2 russet potatoes, peeled and
  diced
1 cup (200 g) split peas
4 cups (1 L) chicken or
  vegetable broth
2 cups (350 g) fresh broccoli
  florets
2 zucchinis, diced
4 cups (200 g) fresh baby
  spinach
5 fresh basil leaves
1 tablespoon lemon juice
Savory Seasoning Blend (page
  12), to taste
Pinch cayenne pepper
  (optional)
Salt and black pepper, to taste

This was a show with a great setting, a great cast of characters, and a great story, which was cut down before it even had time to bloom and grow. I'm not crying, you're crying. I know we all probably have some choice Chinese phrases for whoever made the decision to axe this show, but let's try to focus on the good times, eh browncoats?

Wife Soup was made by *Firefly's* resident badass Zoe, for her whimsical pilot husband, Wash, in the episode "War Stories." Other than the implication that Wife Soup is very tasty, as Wash only gets treated with it when he's "done good," there aren't any details about what's actually in the soup. However, the color was very green and the texture looked smooth and puréed instead of chunky. So, this is a silky-smooth, green vegetable soup—sort of like a cross between split pea and broccoli potato—that can be made vegetarian or not, depending on your whim. This recipe will feed the whole shindig!

1. In a soup pot with a lid, warm the olive oil or butter over medium-high heat. Once the oil is hot, add the onion and sprinkle with the 1 teaspoon of salt. Stir the onion until it begins to turn translucent, 3-4 minutes.

2. Add the celery to the onion and stir. Add the 1 teaspoon of black pepper and continue cooking for another 5-6 minutes, stirring once every minute, adding the garlic when the celery starts to soften.

3. Add the potatoes, split peas, and broth. Bring the soup to a boil, then reduce the heat to a simmer. Cover the soup and simmer for about 1 hour, or until the potatoes and peas are softened.

4. Stir in the broccoli and zucchini. Simmer for 20 more minutes, or until the broccoli is tender. Stir in the spinach and basil, and remove from the heat.

5. Purée the soup in a blender or food processor. Once thoroughly puréed, stir in the lemon juice and add the seasoning blend, cayenne (if using), and the salt and pepper to taste.

MAIN
DISHES

BACON PANCAKES

MAKES 10 PANCAKES

Adventure Time was an animated series on Cartoon Network that follows Jake the Dog and Finn the Human in their wacky adventures in the land of Ooo. It began as an animated short that went viral and eventually became its own series. *Adventure Time* makes frequent references to video games, epic fantasies, and other geeky stuff. Though the target audience is primarily children, *Adventure Time* appeals to children and adults alike . . . especially adults who feel like they are just really tall kids.

One of the many fun and unique things about the show is the music. This particular gem of a recipe comes from a little ditty called, yep, you guessed it, "Bacon Pancakes," written by Rebecca Sugar. It is sung by Jake the Dog during the episode "Burning Low" as he makes breakfast. The concept of bacon pancakes is pretty simple: you take some bacon and put it in a pancake, and then top the cakes with some maple syrup for a breakfast that is truly mathematical!

INGREDIENTS

1 cup (120 g) flour
2 tablespoons sugar
1 teaspoon baking powder
Pinch baking soda
2 tablespoons butter, melted,
   plus extra for frying
¾ cup (180 g) buttermilk
1 egg
10 strips of bacon, fried until
   crispy
Pinch salt
Maple syrup, for serving

1. Combine the flour, sugar, baking powder, and baking soda in a medium bowl.

2. In a separate large bowl, whisk together the 2 tablespoons of butter and the buttermilk, then whisk in the egg.

3. Tip the dry ingredients into the bowl with the wet ingredients and whisk together until it is lump-free.

4. Prepare a large skillet by melting some butter over medium-high heat to prevent the batter from sticking, then add as many bacon strips as you can put in the skillet with enough distance between each one to add the pancake batter. You will probably have to do this in batches.

5. Pour the pancake batter down the length of each bacon strip until it is covered. Make sure the batter around one bacon strip does not touch the batter covering a neighboring strip of bacon—you want them to be individual pancakes and rectangular-ish.

6. Cook until the pancake batter starts to bubble on the surface, then flip them over and brown the other side. Repeat until there are no more slices of bacon. Drizzle with maple syrup and serve. Defiance.

SHAWARMA

SERVES 4–6

This one appeared in the 2012 film version of Marvel's beloved comic series *The Avengers*. The shawarma joke actually has an awesome double-geek meaning. At the end of Nicholas Brenden's audition for the role of Xander in *Buffy the Vampire Slayer*, he asked everybody out for shawarma. Joss Whedon found it hilarious, and the gesture may have ultimately landed him the role. Over a decade later, Tony Stark casually invites the rest of the Avengers out for shawarma after saving New York from an extraterrestrial invasion. After the film's credits, you can see the exhausted Avengers quietly enjoying a shawarma together in a local New York joint.

After watching *The Avengers*, I went out and tried some shawarma from a local eatery and was much delighted. Shawarma is an Arabic meat preparation, involving roasting meats on a vertical spit for hours. Shavings of the meat are cut and stuffed into a pocket of pita bread with various veggies and sauces. Despite not having access to a spit at home, there are a few ways of making a decent homemade shawarma. Soon you'll be chowing down on some just like Thor in *The Avengers*. Seriously, watch it again. He is loving it.

INGREDIENTS

CHICKEN

1 pound (454 g) boneless,
  skinless chicken breast
1 pound (454 g) boneless,
  skinless chicken thighs
¼ cup (60 ml) olive oil
6 cloves garlic, minced
2 teaspoons ground cumin
1 teaspoon curry powder
1 teaspoon paprika
1 teaspoon turmeric
1 teaspoon allspice
Pinch cayenne pepper
Salt and pepper, to taste

SAUCE

¾ cup (175 g) plain Greek yogurt
½ cup (120 g) tahini
¼ cup (60 ml) lemon juice
2 cloves garlic, minced
2 green onions, finely chopped
2 teaspoons ground cumin
Salt and pepper, to taste
1-2 tablespoons olive oil,
  for frying

PITA ASSEMBLY

4 large or 8 small pitas
Thinly sliced red onions,
  to taste
Thinly sliced tomatoes, to taste
Thinly sliced cucumber,
  to taste

1. **To make the chicken:** Slice the chicken breasts and thighs into 2-inch-thick (5 cm) strips and put them in a large bowl. Add the remaining chicken ingredients and combine, making sure the chicken pieces are evenly coated with oil and spices.

2. Transfer the coated chicken to a large resealable plastic bag and leave to marinate in the fridge for as long as possible—preferably overnight, but for at least 2 hours.

3. Preheat the oven to 400°F (200°C). Place the chicken on an aluminum foil-lined baking sheet and roast for about 15 minutes, turning the pieces over halfway through the cooking time. Remove the chicken from the oven and let it rest for a few minutes. Meanwhile, make the sauce.

4. **To make the sauce:** Thoroughly combining all the sauce ingredients in a bowl. Set aside.

5. Thinly slice the cooked chicken. Heat the olive oil in a large skillet, add the sliced chicken, and sauté until it turns brown and crisp on the edges. Make sure not to overcrowd the pan—you may have to do this in batches. You can add some additional spices (from the chicken ingredients) at this point if you like things spicier.

6. **To assemble the pita:** If desired, lightly grill your pitas for about a minute on each side. Open the pita and evenly spread the sauce inside, then fill the pocket with the chicken, onions, tomatoes, and cucumber as you prefer. Enjoy!

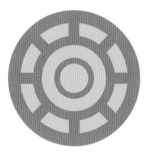

SINNER'S SANDWICH

MAKES 1 SANDWICH

Deadly Premonition is definitely a unique experience. There's a lot of depth and variety to this video game, but there are also a lot of things that don't make sense. The latter adds to the charm for fans of the game . . . and alienates a good amount of other people. It's been described as a good bad game, and I think that sums it up pretty well.

This sandwich appears in an optional cutscene in the A&G Diner, wherein Harry Stewart stops by to order it while York (the protagonist of the game) and Emily are having lunch. York originally thinks Mr. Stewart is eating this bizarre sandwich to punish himself, but, using rhymes and the frequent repeating of "so says Mr. Stewart," York is persuaded to give it a try. Surprisingly, or maybe unsurprisingly, York loves it.

Eating this sandwich is actually a lot like playing *Deadly Premonition* in that you feel like you shouldn't like it because it doesn't make any sense, but you kinda do anyway because it's strangely addictive. The flavor combination is similar to the iconic Thanksgiving sandwich— similar in much the same way *Deadly Premonition* is similar to *Twin Peaks*—yet it's somehow even more bizarre. I recommend adding a bit of heat for some extra punishment. That seems like a good idea, doesn't it, Zach? My coffee says so.

INGREDIENTS

Spicy chipotle sandwich spread
 or spicy mayo (optional)
2 slices white bread
⅛ pound or 2 ounces (50 g)
 cooked turkey slices
Arugula, to taste
1–2 slices pepper jack cheese
1 tablespoon strawberry jam
¼ cup (7 g) Chex cereal

1. Smear the spicy sandwich spread of your choice onto one of the slices of white bread.

2. Top the spread with the turkey slices.

3. Scatter the arugula over the turkey.

4. Place the cheese on top of the arugula.

5. On the other slice of bread, spread the strawberry jam.

6. Press the Chex on top of the jam.

7. At this point, you can choose whether to eat the sandwich with the cereal and jam on top, as it appears in most of the cutscenes, or you can face that piece down and enjoy it how it appears when York actually eats it.

8. Atone for your sins.

BULGAR ASHKHAN

SERVES 5-6

Defiance was a show on the Syfy network with a corresponding MMORPG. It takes place around thirty years in the future after a bunch of alien races have arrived on Earth and terraformed the entire planet. The story follows the humans and aliens coexisting in a town called Defiance, formerly St. Louis, Missouri. Defiance exists independently of the Earth Republic, which controls the majority of what was once North America. Because the town does not exclude any type, it is a melting pot of alien races, who all bring their own cultural influences, including food.

Bulgar Ashkhan is a traditional dish of the Castithan race—a race who are pale and nice to look at but have a tendency to be arrogant and self-serving. The dish is seen in the season 1 episode "Brothers in Arms," when it is prepared for alien mob boss and quasi-villain Datak Tar. It looks like pink oatmeal but is clearly savory, given the identifiable ingredients shown on the preparation table: red chili, bell pepper, and spices. When I first heard the characters say "Bulgar Ashkhan," I thought they were referring to actual bulgur (the wheat), so I have included that in the ingredients and made a sort of spicy pink curry. No shtako, it is delicious!

INGREDIENTS

1 red onion, chopped
3 cloves garlic, minced
Butter or oil, for sautéing
1 large red bell pepper, seeded and chopped
1-2 red chilies, seeded and chopped
1 pound (454 g) ground pow (pork)
10 fresh basil leaves, whole
2 tablespoons fish sauce
1 cup (140 g) bulgur, cooked and drained
2 tablespoons red curry paste
1½ cups (355 ml) coconut milk
Beet juice or pink food coloring (for color)

1. In a large skillet, sauté the onion and garlic in oil or butter over medium-high heat until the onions are translucent.

2. Add the bell pepper and chili, and sauté for 5 more minutes.

3. Add the ground pork, basil, and fish sauce to the veggies, and stir to combine, breaking up the pork. Cook until the meat is no longer pink.

4. Tip the cooked bulgur into the pork mixture and combine thoroughly, continuing to sauté over medium–low heat.

5. Stir in the red curry paste—it should evenly coat everything in the pan—then add the coconut milk and stir some more.

6. Let simmer, uncovered, for about 10 minutes. Add the beet juice or food coloring right before you're planning to serve and stir to make sure the color is evenly dispersed.

HASPERAT

MAKES 2 HASPERAT

Hasperat has appeared in three *Star Trek* series: *Voyager*, *TNG*, and most often in *DS9*. It's a traditional Bajoran dish, made from a brine that is known for being spicy enough to make one's eyes water and figuratively set the mouth on fire. I felt the need to clarify "figuratively" because this is *Star Trek* we're talking about—anything can and does happen. Hasperat is mentioned (and eaten) pretty often in *Deep Space 9*, as this particular series takes place in Bajoran territory. It is also a favorite of *TNG*'s Ensign Ro, whose father made an especially strong Hasperat.

Hasperat generally appears as a wrap or burrito and is eaten with the hands. So, this recipe is for a grilled wrap with hot pickled veggies (for the brined element) and hot sauce, complemented by cheese, avocado, and onions. It will make your eyes water and will definitely sear your tongue, but it will be so tasty, you'll happily endure the pain. This makes for a wonderful light lunch or an on-the-go meal to take to the holodeck or on an away mission outside your home after watching *Star Trek* all day.

INGREDIENTS

2 large tortillas
½ cup or 4 ounces (115 g)
   cream cheese
Hot sauce of your choice,
   to taste
½ cup or 2 ounces (55 g)
   shredded Monterey Jack
   cheese
¼ avocado, peeled, destoned,
   and thinly sliced
½ red onion, chopped
½ cup (70 g) chopped hot
   pickled vegetables
¼ cup (15 g) spinach or
   arugula leaves

1. Zap (or phaser) your tortillas in the microwave on high, covered with a damp piece of paper towel, for a few seconds so they are pliable.

2. In a small bowl, mix the cream cheese with the desired amount of hot sauce. Spread this mixture on your tortillas, making sure to completely cover them—this is what's going to hold the wrap together.

3. Layer the cheese on top, then top with the avocado, onion, spinach or arugula, and hot pickled vegetables.

4. Tightly roll the tortillas and tuck in the ends. If you wish, you can lightly grill them on each side for a few minutes.

5. Cut each wrap in half diagonally and serve.

ROCK SIRLOIN

SERVES 1–2

Rock Sirloin or Sirloin Rocks has been mentioned or appeared in three *Zelda* games: *OoT*, *MM*, and *TP*. It is a "food" item eaten only by the Goron race, whose diet consists solely of rocks. The Rock Sirloin is sort of like the lobster of Goron cuisine: it's fancy. It's only found in Dondongo's Cavern, making it a rare and somewhat dangerous delicacy. In *Majora's Mask*, getting a Rock Sirloin is necessary to obtain one of the game's many masks.

Rock Sirloin appears as rocks in the shape of a cut of meat that only seems to exist in Japanese cartoons. I imagine that Goron's Rock Sirloin is crunchy on the outside and filled with a tender earthy-meaty flavor on the inside. So, I made a simplified but incredibly tasty version of a beef Wellington, which is tender beef coated with duxelles and wrapped in a crispy, buttery puff pastry, which just so happens to look like a rock when cooked. The flavor is both earthy and rich. Draw yourself a bath, put on "Saria's Song," and pretend you're a Goron luxuriating in a hot spring while eating a delicious Rock Sirloin.

INGREDIENTS

12 medium mushrooms
4 shallots, peeled and diced
Chopped fresh thyme, to taste
3 tablespoons butter, divided
Salt and pepper, to taste
¼ cup (60 ml) sherry
6 ounces (170 g) high-quality
   steak, cut into two equal-size
   pieces
1 sheet ready-made puff pastry,
   thawed
2-3 slices prosciutto

1. Preheat the oven to 350°F (180°C).

2. Finely mince the mushrooms in a food processor.

3. In a large skillet, melt 1 tablespoon of the butter and cook the mushrooms, shallots, and thyme, seasoned with salt and pepper, until they begin to brown.

4. Add another tablespoon of butter to the skillet and, when melted, add the sherry. Sauté until all the liquid is absorbed, then remove the pan from heat and set aside to cool.

5. Wrap each piece of steak in twine to make a round shape. Season with salt and pepper.

6. In a hot pan over high heat, brown both pieces of steak in the remaining 1 tablespoon butter for 1–1½ minutes on each side. When done, remove the twine and let the meat rest.

7. Unroll the puff pastry sheet and layer on the prosciutto, then the mushroom mixture. In the center of the pastry sheet, place both pieces of meat, side by side.

8. Fold the pastry over the meat to create a figure eight or infinity shape. Cut off any excess dough.

9. Bake on a parchment-lined cookie sheet for 15–20 minutes, or until the pastry is a flaky golden brown.

10. Remove from the oven and skewer either end with corn skewers. Enjoy!

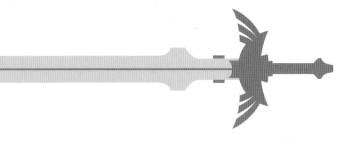

BIG KAHUNA BURGER

MAKES 6–8 BURGERS

Quentin Tarantino's films are not everyone's cup of homicidal tea, but they have a strong cult following and are widely acknowledged for their memorable characters, excellent dialogue, and well-choreographed violence. Personally, I am a huge fan. The fictional burger joint Big Kahuna Burger is mentioned in several of Quentin Tarantino's films, but the most memorable reference occurs in the classic *Pulp Fiction*, in the infamous scene when Jules and Vincent bust in on the unfortunate folks who wronged Marcellus Wallace and proceed to eat their burgers and shoot up the place.

So, Big Kahuna Burger is clearly a HA-waiian-themed burger joint, but what Jules appears to be eating in the scene is a typical fast-food burger. I wanted to reconcile those two things so that the burger would taste Hawaiian but look like the generic burger in the scene. I figured, in true fast-food tradition, to put the differentiating element in the patty itself. The patties are made with pineapple and bacon mixed into the beef and coated in teriyaki sauce. Make sure to eat them before eleven in the morning because hamburgers are, in the immortal words of Jules, the cornerstone of any nutritious breakfast, inspired by *Pulp Fiction*.

INGREDIENTS

1 pound (454 g) ground beef
10 slices bacon, cooked crispy
  and crumbled
½ red onion, minced
1 egg
20-ounce (567 g) can crushed
  pineapple, thoroughly drained
2 tablespoons bread crumbs
Salt and pepper, to taste
Teriyaki glaze, to coat
6–8 plain hamburger buns
6–8 slices cheddar cheese
Excessive ketchup
Pickles, tomato, onion, and
  mayo, for serving (optional)
6–8 leaves iceberg lettuce
  (optional)

1. Heat a grill to medium. You can also use a skillet over medium-high heat.

2. In a mixing bowl, combine the ground beef, bacon, onion, egg, crushed pineapple, bread crumbs, and salt and pepper.

3. Form 6–8 meat patties from the mixture—their size will depend on how large the buns are.

4. Coat each patty with the teriyaki glaze.

5. Grill or fry the patties on both sides to the desired doneness.

6. While the patties are cooking, toast the buns.

7. When the patties are done, glaze each one again with more teriyaki, then top with a slice of cheese.

8. Spread some ketchup over the cheese and place the patties on the bottom bun. Load up with any additional burger toppings you want to use, then finish with some lettuce leaves. Close each burger with the top bun and press down.

9. Use the burger as an effective intimidation technique because you are bad . . . and wash down with a tasty beverage—like Sprite!

DEEPER'N'EVER PIE

MAKES 2 PIES

Redwall is one of those series that's just filled with beautiful descriptions of food. Candied chestnuts, dandelion cordials, honey-covered hotcakes, shrimp garnished with cream and rose leaves . . . I couldn't possibly cover all of it. For more scrumptious *Redwall* recipes from the author himself, Brian Jacques, I recommend also adding *The Official Redwall Cookbook* to your nerdy cookbook collection.

Deeper'n'Ever Pie's full title is Deeper'n'Ever Turnip'n'Tater'n'Beetroot Pie. So, for some context, the characters in the *Redwall* series are all anthropomorphic animals (primarily woodland creatures) with cultures, dialects, and dispositions that are determined by animal type. This pie is the favorite dish of the moles, who unsurprisingly enjoy root vegetables. I added cheese and herbs to make a delicious and earthy pie that will hopefully make the moles say, "Boi 'eck, oi loik dis pie, yes zurr! Quoite noice, says oi!"

INGREDIENTS

CRUST
2 cups (240 g) all-purpose flour
Pinch salt
¼ cup or ½ stick (60 g) butter,
    chilled
½ cup (120 ml) ice water
⅓ pound or 5 ounces (140 g)
    grated Gruyère
⅓ pound or 5 ounces (140 g)
    grated smoked Gouda

FILLING
1 cup (240 ml) milk
2 tablespoons butter
4 shallots, peeled and sliced
4 cloves garlic, minced
1 tablespoon chopped fresh
    thyme
1 tablespoon smoked paprika
1 tablespoon nutmeg
Salt and pepper, to taste
1 cup (230 g) sour cream
1 large turnip, boiled, peeled,
    and cut into ¼-inch-thick
    (6 mm) slices
1 golden potato, boiled, peeled,
    and cut into ¼-inch-thick
    (6 mm) slices
1 small beet, boiled, peeled,
    and cut into ¼-inch-thick
    (6 mm) slices
1 pie crust and 1 sheet of pie
    dough for the lid
⅓ pound or 5 ounces (140 g)
    grated Gruyère
⅓ pound or 5 ounces (140 g)
    grated smoked Gouda

1. **To make the crust:** Combine the flour and salt in a large bowl. Cut the butter into small pieces and add it to the flour. Using your fingers, press the butter into the flour until it reaches a crumbly texture. Add the ice water, a little at a time, until the dough binds and can be formed into a ball. Wrap the dough in plastic wrap and refrigerate for at least 2 hours.

2. Preheat the oven to 375°F (190°C). Roll out the dough to fit a 9-inch (23 cm) pie pan. Place the crust in the pan and carefully and evenly press the dough onto its bottom and sides. Trim any excess dough and set aside. Sprinkle a little of both cheeses into the crust to just cover the base.

3. **To make the filling:** Add the milk, butter, shallots, garlic, thyme, paprika, nutmeg, and salt and pepper to a small pan. Simmer until the shallots soften. Remove the milk-shallot mixture from the heat and stir in the sour cream.

4. Cover the cheesy crust with a layer of beets. Spoon some of the creamy shallot sauce over the beets and top with another layer of cheese. On top of the cheese, add a layer of potatoes. Cover the potatoes with a layer of creamy shallot sauce and then more cheese. Add a layer of turnips on top of the potato-sauce-cheese layers and cover with more shallot sauce and cheese.

5. Roll out the remaining dough and cover the pie filling. Press down on the edges to seal, then trim the excess dough.

6. Cut slits in the center of the pie as vents. Bake in the oven for 20 minutes, or until the pie crust is golden and flaky.

GAGH

SERVES 2-4

Klingons: they're fearless warriors but they eat some nasty foods by human standards. Gagh is a popular Klingon dish composed of serpent worms. It is mentioned in *TNG*, *DS9*, and *ENT*. One of my favorite episodes of *TNG* is "A Matter of Honor," in which Riker participates in an officer exchange program and becomes acting commander of a Klingon vessel. A man after my own heart, Riker samples some Klingon cuisine in order to prepare himself for this monumental responsibility, including what looks like a giant octopus, something called Pipius Claw, and, of course, Gagh. Later in the episode, while eating dinner with the members of his Klingon crew, Riker is pressured to eat Gagh how it is supposed to be eaten: alive and wriggling. After being teased a little by the Klingon crew members, Riker eats the Gagh without flinching, which impresses the Klingons. Riker himself is impressed that Klingons are actually capable of humor, having only had Lieutenant Worf as an example of Klingon behavior. Basically, everyone learns more about each other and much bonding ensues. Definitely in my top ten *TNG* episodes.

Gagh comes in different varieties and looks a little different each time it is depicted. I tried to emulate the version from "A Matter of Honor" with some delicious stir-fried noodles. The best part about making this dish is watching as the "worms" squirm when you cook them. That may sound kinda gross, but I assure you, they are delicious. Still, if Klingon food is too strong for you . . .

INGREDIENTS

4 cloves garlic, minced
6 green onions, finely chopped
10 thin slices bacon
4 medium mushrooms, thinly
  sliced
1 cup (70 g) shredded cabbage
1 bouillon cube
3 cups (750 ml) water
4–6 tablespoons soy sauce
Hot sauce of your choice
  (I used sriracha), to taste
8 ounces (227 g) udon noodles
5 ounces (140 g) regular or
  dried spinach fettuccine
  noodles
4–5 drops red food coloring
  (optional)
Lemon juice, to taste

1. In a large, deep pan over medium-high heat, sauté the garlic, onions, and bacon for a couple of minutes. Add the mushrooms and cabbage, and sauté for a couple more minutes, combining everything.

2. Crumble in the bouillon cube, pour in the water, and let everything simmer for 5 minutes.

3. Add the soy and hot sauces and cook, stirring, for about 1 minute. Stir in the udon and fettuccine noodles so that they separate and mix in with the other ingredients.

4. Add a few drops of red food coloring (if using) and stir to spread evenly.

5. Cook until most of the liquid is absorbed and the noodles are soft.

6. When serving, squeeze a bit of lemon juice over the noodles.

LOS POLLOS HERMANOS CHICKEN

SERVES 2

Yo, yo, yo! 1-4-8-3 to the 3 to the 6 to the 9. Representin' the ABQ! This offering is from everyone's favorite fictional fast-food joint that's actually a cover for a giant meth operation, Los Pollos Hermanos. Unlike most drug fronts, Los Pollos Hermanos, a chain of fast-food restaurants specializing in fried chicken, are actually quality establishments. This is because Gustavo Fring, the owner, is as meticulous in the running of his restaurant operation as he is in the running of his meth operation. It's almost as if there aren't large amounts of meth hidden in the barrels of fry batter.

The chicken at Los Pollos Hermanos has a Latin flare, so this is some flavorful and spicy fried chicken. As always with deep frying, you'll probably end up in a sticky situation, and may need to call for help (dial 505-503-4455!). While you will certainly get dirty, the means justify the ends. With a spicy, crispy exterior and a tender interior, I think you'll find that this chicken tastes much better than roof pizza.

INGREDIENTS

½ cup (120 ml) lime juice
½ cup (120 ml) orange juice
8 ounces (227 g) sour cream
2 cloves garlic, minced
1 teaspoon chili powder,
  divided
1 teaspoon ground cumin,
  divided
Cayenne pepper, to taste
Savory Seasoning Blend (page
  12), to taste
1 teaspoon dried oregano
Salt and black pepper, to taste
4 chicken tenders
2 large eggs
Hot sauce, to taste (optional)
1 cup (125 g) all-purpose flour
1 cup (120 g) corn flour
High-smoke-point oil or lard,
  for deep frying

1. Combine the lime juice, orange juice, sour cream, minced garlic, ½ teaspoon each of the chili powder and ground cumin, the cayenne and seasoning blend to taste, the oregano, and some salt and pepper in a nonreactive bowl.

2. Add the chicken tenders and toss to coat. Let the chicken marinate in the fridge, covered, for at least 2 hours, but overnight is best. When ready to cook, let the chicken sit at room temperature for about 20 minutes before breading.

3. In a bowl, whisk together the eggs and the hot sauce (if using) until the mixture turns bright orange. In a separate bowl, sift together both flours, the remaining chili powder and ground cumin and the cayenne, seasoning blend, and salt and pepper to taste.

4. Set up a deep fryer with the frying oil of your choice, then heat the oil to 350°F (190°C). You may also use a cast-iron skillet or other high-temperature pot for frying.

5. Dip the marinated chicken in the egg mixture, and then coat well in the flour mixture.

6. Fry the chicken in the oil until it is brown and crisp, 8–10 minutes. You may need to do this in batches depending on the size of your deep fryer or pot. Use tongs to turn the chicken to make sure it is getting fried evenly, gently rotating it occasionally.

7. Place the fried chicken on a wire rack or paper towel to rest for about 10 minutes before serving.

MABEL'S PASTIES

MAKES 4 PASTIES

Neil Gaiman's *American Gods* is one of my all-time favorite books. Full disclosure: I spent much of my teen years holed up in my room reading and rereading Neil Gaiman books and comics. Out of all of Neil Gaiman's fantastic novels, *American Gods* spoke to me the most. It follows Shadow Moon, an ex-convict who, after being released from prison, finds himself plunged into the middle of a very strange war between the gods of our ancestors and new gods we've created for ourselves in America.

Somewhere in the middle of the book, Shadow spends a few months lying low in the fictional, almost-too-nice town of Lakeside, Wisconsin. In Lakeside, the local eatery is run by the very gregarious Mabel, who is "famous" for her pasties. As mentioned in the novel, pasties made their way to Michigan's Upper Peninsula area in the 1800s along with the influx of Cornish miners, and now the area sees more than a few bastardized versions of the traditional hand pie. Shadow describes Mabel's pasties as "a savory delight wrapped in hot pastry" and notes that they contain meat, potatoes, carrots, and onions. I don't know about you, but chances are that if you stick that in pie crust, I will like it. Enjoy these bad boys at breakfast with some hot chocolate and the local morning paper, which may or may not have a missing children's section.

INGREDIENTS

1 large russet potato, peeled and chopped small
2 carrots, peeled and finely chopped
½ yellow onion, chopped
1 pound (454 g) lean ground beef
Savory Seasoning Blend (page 12), to taste
Salt and black pepper, to taste
2 Double-Crust Pie Dough (page 13)

1. Preheat the oven to 350°F (180°C).

2. In a large bowl, add all the ingredients—except the pie dough—and mix together.

3. Separate the dough into 4 equal pieces and roll each piece into a 6-inch (15 cm) circle.

4. Add the filling to the center of each pie disk. Fold the disks over to create semicircular pockets. Wet your fingers and crimp the edges together to seal. Cut small slits into the center of the dough to vent.

5. Place the pies on a parchment-lined baking sheet and bake for 35–40 minutes, or until the dough is golden brown.

HIGHLAND SANDWICHES

SERVES 4

To some minds, the whole icky romance thing takes *Outlander* firmly out of geek territory. However, if we can collectively pretend that the bodice-ripping element doesn't exist, *Outlander* is essentially a fantasy story about time travel, which is unambiguously geeky. Not only that, but the screen adaption is headed by none other than Ronald D. Moore of *Star Trek* and *Battlestar Galactica* fame.

Much of the *Outlander* series takes place in the Scottish Highlands, so the culture of eighteenth-century Scotland is a huge part of the story's setting, including the cuisine. Bannocks, brose, and haggis are just some of the traditional foods that make an appearance. One tasty-sounding treat, which has roots in Scottish tradition but is mostly unique to the *Outlander* series, is what the protagonist, Claire, calls a Highland Sandwich. Appearing in the third book, it is described as a loaf of freshly baked bread stuffed with sheep's cheese and homemade pickle. For the fresh bread, I opted for Scottish baps, or morning rolls, which lend themselves perfectly to sandwiches, with Scottish chutney and fresh sheep cheese.

INGREDIENTS

PICKLE/CHUTNEY

2 medium yellow onions,
  peeled and finely chopped
2 McIntosh apples, peeled,
  cored, and roughly chopped
¼ cup (37 g) raisins, sultanas,
  and/ or currants
2 teaspoons peeled and grated
  fresh ginger
¾ cup (170 g) packed light
  brown sugar
½ cup (120 ml) malt vinegar
½ cup (120 ml) apple cider
  vinegar
3 teaspoons Sweet Spice Blend
  (page 12), or to taste
Salt and black pepper, to taste
1 sterilized canning jar

BAPS

2 tablespoons butter
1¾ cups (220 g) bread flour,
  plus extra for dusting
2½ teaspoons fresh yeast
1 teaspoon granulated sugar
½ cup (120 ml) milk, room
  temperature, plus extra for
  brushing
½ teaspoon salt

Fresh sheep's milk cheese*,
  to taste

1. **To make the pickle/chutney (Note: This will need at least a week or two to mature.):** Place all the pickle ingredients (except the jar!) into a large pan. Bring slowly to a boil and then reduce the heat to a rolling boil. Stir the chutney regularly and make sure it does not burn. Cook until it is the consistency of a thick jam and all the liquids have dissolved. Spoon the hot pickle into a hot and sterile jar (you can either boil the jar or use the sterilize feature on a dishwasher) and seal immediately. Store in a cool, dark place and leave to mature for at least a week.

2. **To make the baps:** Rub the butter into the flour, then make a well in the center. In a small mixing bowl, mix the yeast with the sugar, then add the milk and salt, and let sit for a few minutes. Then pour the yeast mixture into the well.

3. Mix until it forms a dough, adding extra warm milk, if required. Cover the dough with plastic wrap or a light cloth and allow to rise until doubled in size, for about an hour or two depending on the temperature of your kitchen.

4. Knead the dough and then evenly divide it into 4 pieces. Knead each piece into a ball about the size of a fist, flatten with your hand, and then lightly roll into a round with a rolling pin. Place the dough balls on a well-floured baking tray. Brush with milk and sprinkle flour all over the tops. Allow to rise for another 20 minutes. Preheat the oven to 400°F (200°C).

5. Bake for 10 minutes, or until golden brown and firm to the touch. Dust with more flour and allow them to cool a bit on a wire rack.

6. Time to assemble the sandwich! Cut a bap in half horizontally from the middle. Spread the sheep's cheese over the bottom half and top with the relish. Finish the sandwich with the top half of the bap. Repeat for each bap. Enjoy!

* Fresh sheep's milk cheese is seasonal and difficult to find. There are several online retailers that sell it, or try grocery stores that sell local or specialty cheeses. If you absolutely cannot find it, thoroughly mix together ricotta with chèvre, at a 2:1 ratio, and you'll have an acceptable approximation.

BEEF AND BACON PIE

SERVES 2-4

For my blog and cookbooks, I try to only take on a very select few dishes from this series—a "best of," if you will. I generally aim for the big, obvious ones that are memorable enough to be mentioned in HBO's *Game of Thrones*. For this one, though, there is no special reason for its inclusion other than I just wanted to make it. I mean, it's beef . . . and bacon . . . pie. Not to jump on the old bacon hype train, but I'm pretty much doing that. Beef and Bacon Pie sounds amazing. Like (SPOILERS!) Joffrey getting poisoned at his own wedding amazing. Maybe even Drogon crashing into Meereen's fighting pits and looking at Daenerys like "get in!" amazing. Sansa's revenge amazing? I could go on . . .

The most memorable appearance of this pie is when Jon Snow is fleeing the wall to try to join up with Robb Stark after the death of Eddard Stark. Feeling particularly homesick, he wishes he could hear Bran's laugh or one of Old Nan's stories, or eat one of Gage's (the head cook of Winterfell) Beef and Bacon Pies. So, let's try Jon Snow's comfort food of choice.

INGREDIENTS

1 pound (454 g) stew beef,
  cubed
Salt and black pepper, to taste
2 tablespoons olive oil
10 strips thick-cut bacon, diced
2 carrots, roughly chopped
1 yellow onion, chopped
1 cup (240 ml) red wine
1 cup (240 ml) beef broth
1 cup (150 g) raisins
2 bay leaves
1 teaspoon chopped fresh
  thyme
½ teaspoon ground allspice
1 Double-Crust Pie Dough
  (page 13)
1 tablespoon flour, for dusting

1. Preheat the oven to 325°F (170°C).

2. Season the beef with the salt and pepper. In a Dutch oven, brown the beef in the olive oil until it gets some good color on all sides. Remove and set aside.

3. Add the bacon to the Dutch oven and cook until crispy. Remove with a slotted spoon and set the bacon aside, leaving the fat behind.

4. Add the carrots to the bacon fat and sauté until they are softened, then add the onion. Keep cooking until the onion is soft and beginning to caramelize.

5. Add back the beef, along with the red wine, beef broth, raisins, herbs, and spices. Use a wooden spoon to scrape up any brown bits sticking to the pot and incorporate them with the broth and wine.

6. Cover the Dutch oven with the lid and transfer it to the oven to braise for 1–2 hours, or until the beef is tender enough that it can be mashed with a fork. Break the beef up into smaller pieces—this will help incorporate the gravy. Once done, stir in the bacon.

7. Increase the oven temperature to 375°F (190°C).

8. Roll out the pie dough on a lightly floured surface. Grease and line two 12-ounce (340 g) ramekins with pie dough, keeping in mind that there should be enough dough left over to top them as well. Trim away the excess.

9. Spoon the beef mixture into each dough-lined ramekin, rationing it evenly between the pies.

10. Roll out the remaining dough again and top each of the ramekins with a layer of dough, cutting off any excess and rerolling as necessary. Crimp the edges of the pie to seal and cut vents into the center.

11. Bake the pies for about 25 minutes, or until the crust is golden brown.

DOUBLEMEAT MEDLEY

MAKES 2 MEDLEYS

Buffy the Vampire Slayer is absolutely beloved by its fans. We all wished we could be part of the Scooby Gang: reading big tomes, casting spells, staking vamps, and just generally saving the world a lot. Expanding on the horror-comedy film of the same name, the *BtVS* series took the story of the vampire slayer (a young girl chosen to fight the forces of evil) to a whole new level. The show was a game changer for fantasy horror–based television, slaying all expectations while effortlessly walking the tightrope of being terrifying, poignant, and wickedly funny—sometimes all at once.

In the most painful season, the Slayer is forced to face a new beast: the minimum-wage fast-food job. It doesn't take long for Buffy to sense that there's something weird going on at the Doublemeat Palace. Employees periodically disappear and there's a mysterious ingredient described only as a "meat process." Naturally, Buffy assumes her coworkers are becoming the secret ingredient. However, the truth is, while her coworkers are being eaten by a demon, the "meat" at the Doublemeat Palace is actually just processed vegetables. I give you, The Doublemeat Medley: a classic double-decker with a twist. A veggie-beef patty above the mid-bun and a slice of veggie-chicken product below the mid-bun. Plus pickles!

INGREDIENTS

"CHICKEN" PATTY

8 ounces (227 g) extra-firm
   tofu, drained and crumbled
½ tablespoon white miso
½ tablespoon soy sauce
½ teaspoon chicken-style
   seasoning
Savory Seasoning Blend (page
   12), to taste
Salt and black pepper, to taste

"BEEF" PATTY

8 ounces (227 g) veggie ground
   beef
½ tablespoon nutritional yeast
3 tablespoons breadcrumbs
Dash Worcestershire sauce
3 tablespoons onion, minced
Savory Seasoning Blend (page
   12), to taste
Salt and black pepper, to taste
1 tablespoon cornstarch
Oil of choice, for cooking

BURGER ASSEMBLY

Ketchup
Mustard
Mayo
4 sesame seed buns
Sandwich sliced pickles
Thinly sliced white onion
Green leaf lettuce leaves
Sliced cheese
Sliced hothouse tomato

1. **To make the "chicken" patty:** Combine all the chicken patty ingredients in a food processor or in a bowl using an immersion blender.

2. Line a colander with cheesecloth. Scoop the tofu mixture into the cheesecloth and wrap it up. Place a plate on the bundle and add a heavy object (like a big can of something) on top. Put the colander into a large bowl and refrigerate for at least 4 hours, but overnight is best. This allows the tofu to drain and the flavors to permeate.

3. Preheat the oven to 375°F (190°C) and line a baking sheet with parchment paper.

4. Scoop out the tofu mixture and form into 2 disks or patties. Bake on the prepared baking sheet for 20 minutes, or until lightly browned. Meanwhile, make the "beef" patty.

5. **To make the "beef" patty:** Mix together all the beef patty ingredients—except the cooking oil—in a bowl, then form into 2 patties.

6. Heat some oil in a skillet over medium-high heat. Cook the patties for 3 minutes on each side, or until they have a nice color on the outside.

7. **To assemble the sandwich:** Spread the condiments on the bottom part of the bun. In this order, top the bun base with pickles, onions, a lettuce leaf, a chicken patty, and cheese. Top with more condiments.

8. On top of the chicken patty with condiments, place another bottom bun. On this bun spread some condiments, followed by a lettuce leaf, a slice of tomato, and then a beef patty. Top the beef patty with condiments and finish with the top bun. Repeat the process for the other burger.

HERRING AND PUMPKIN POT PIE

SERVES 6-8

INGREDIENTS

2 tablespoons unsalted butter

2 tablespoons all-purpose flour, plus extra for dusting

1¼ cups (300 ml) whole milk, heated to 100–110°F (38–43°C)

Salt and black pepper, to taste

Olive or vegetable oil, for frying

1 white onion, chopped

1 kabocha pumpkin, steamed and peeled

3 ounces (75 g) smoked herring fillets*, drained and fillets chopped very small

2 Double-Crust Pie Dough (page 13)

2 cups (230 g) shredded sharp white cheddar cheese

10 black olives

* Let's face it, many people find the taste and texture of herring gross. That's okay; it's an acquired taste. If you can't stomach the thought of herring, hot smoked salmon will do nicely instead.

Kiki's Delivery Service is the Studio Ghibli film based on the book *Majo no Takkyu bin* by Eiko Kadono, which was adapted and directed by Hayao Miyazaki in 1989. Studio Ghibli is now famous worldwide for its beautiful animations but at the time it gained some attention for its delicious depictions of food, which are absolutely mouthwatering. Let's be real, if I was in *Spirited Away*, I probably would have gone on a gluttony-fueled rampage like No-Face and/or suffered the same fate as Chihiro's parents and regretted nothing.

Kiki's Delivery Service has less food moments than some other Ghibli films, but it does have an awesome talking cat and this very memorable pie. In the film, Kiki is a witch, and witches eventually leave their hometowns to find their very own towns to serve and protect, using their unique witchy abilities. Kiki's only known ability is flying, so when she finds her town, she finds herself offering a delivery service. One of her customers is a sweet, old lady who needs Kiki's help delivering a herring and pumpkin pot pie to her granddaughter's birthday party. Herring is definitely an acquired taste, but the pie looks warm and comforting, is dotted with black olives, and has a little fish design in the dough.

1. Melt the butter in a heavy-bottomed saucepan. Stir in the flour and cook over medium heat, stirring constantly, until it bubbles—but don't let it get brown—around 2 minutes.

2. Add the milk, stirring as the sauce thickens. Bring to a boil, add the salt and pepper to taste, reduce the heat, and cook, stirring, for 2–3 minutes more. Remove from the heat and set aside.

3. Put some oil in a skillet and sauté the onion until it is aromatic and translucent. Cut the pumpkin into largish chunks, add salt and pepper, and then briefly sauté them with the onion so they absorb some flavor.

4. Add the chopped fillets and the sauce to the pumpkin and onion, and stir everything together. You don't want to mix; instead, stir enough to coat everything in the sauce. Season again with salt and pepper, or any other seasoning that takes your fancy.

5. On a floured surface, roll out about half the dough so it's big enough to cover a standard rectangular casserole dish. Grease the casserole dish and line it with the rolled-out dough. Cut off the excess and set aside.

6. Spoon the pumpkin-herring mixture into the pastry-lined casserole dish. Spread it out so it evenly covers the surface. Sprinkle the white cheddar on top of the mixture so it covers it as much as possible.

7. Roll out the remaining dough and cover the top. Puncture the dough all over with something sharp and pointy to create vents. You should have a good amount of dough left over, which will be used to make the design. Preheat the oven to 375°F (190°C).

8. For the decorating, I highly recommend looking at a picture of the pie online or pausing the film. Take the leftover dough and roll it out again. Cut 5–6 strips from it, about an inch (2.5 cm) or so wide. Place them on top of the pie, diagonally, one at a time, with some space in between to create the water design. Cut off the excess. On the end of each strip, place a black olive and push it into the dough a bit.

9. Cut a fish shape from the rolled-out dough. Place that in the center of the pie on top of the lines. Using whatever dough is left over, add the fins, eyes, mouth, and "scales." Use a knife to create the indents on the tail and fins.

10. Bake the pie for about 25 minutes, or until the top crust is golden brown but not burnt. Use your oven light to check on the pie periodically to make sure it's not burning. You did it!

LOIN SERVED WITH A CUMBERLAND SAUCE OF RED FRUITS

SERVES 4-6

The *Hannibal* series is a rare instance of an adaption that actually adds to its source material. I've been a huge fan of the Thomas Harris books and the films for quite some time, but the TV show took the series to new, even more disturbing places. Not only that, it's taken Hannibal's food game well beyond fava beans and Chianti (or Amarone, for book fans).

There are three important things to remember about Hannibal Lecter: he hates rude people; he can manipulate a person to eat their own face; he has very expensive taste. He often uses ingredients that are, shall we say, difficult to obtain? In the TV series, Hannibal has served his friends and acquaintances everything from black chicken soup to blood puddings, and, of course, their own appendages. I chose this dish, from the season 1 episode "Amuse-Bouche," for its relative simplicity. Hannibal tells Crawford that the "loin" is served in "a Cumberland sauce of red fruits." Of course, the "loin" is really, definitely, going to be pork this time.

INGREDIENTS

PORK LOIN
¼ cup (60 ml) extra-virgin
 olive oil
¼ cup (60 ml) soy sauce
2 cloves garlic, minced
3 tablespoons Dijon honey
 mustard
Savory Seasoning Blend (page
 12), to taste
Salt and black pepper, to taste
1-2 pounds (454-907 g)
 boneless pork loin roast, on
 the thicker side

SAUCE
1 orange
1 lemon
⅔ cup (200 g) red currant jelly*
½ cup (120 ml) port wine
1 tablespoon red wine vinegar
½ teaspoon mustard powder
½ teaspoon ground ginger
½ teaspoon cornstarch
Salt and black pepper, to taste

SIDE
1 shallot, minced
2 teaspoons Dijon mustard
2 tablespoons white wine vinegar
½ cup (120 ml) extra-virgin
 olive oil
Salt and black pepper, to taste
1 pound (454 g) haricot vert or
 green beans, lightly steamed
½ cup (25 g) Bleu d'Auvergne or
 other blue cheese, crumbled
¼ cup (30 g) walnuts, toasted

1. **To make the pork:** Whisk together the olive oil, soy sauce, garlic, mustard, seasoning blend, and salt and pepper in a bowl. Place the pork loin in a large resealable plastic bag and pour in the marinade. Marinate in the refrigerator at least 1 hour.

2. **To make the sauce:** Zest the orange and lemon. Place the fruit rinds in a medium saucepan and cover with some water. Bring to a boil over medium-high heat, then reduce the heat to medium and simmer, stirring occasionally, for 5 minutes, or until the rinds soften. Drain the liquid, but keep the rinds.

3. Squeeze the juice from the orange and lemon and add it to the rinds with the jelly, wine, vinegar, mustard powder, and ginger. Cook, stirring, over medium heat for 3-5 minutes. Reduce the heat to low and simmer, stirring occasionally, for 6-8 minutes, or until the sauce thickens slightly.

4. Combine the cornstarch and a couple tablespoons of water. Add the cornstarch mixture to the sauce and cook, stirring constantly, over medium heat, for about a minute, or until the mixture thickens slightly. Season with the salt and pepper. Transfer to a heatproof serving jug and let cool to about room temperature.

5. Preheat the oven to 350°F (180°C).

6. Transfer the pork loin to a baking dish and pour the marinade over the pork. Cook in the oven until the pork is no longer pink in the center, 45-60 minutes. A meat thermometer inserted into the center should read 145°F (62°C). Let the pork rest while make the side.

7. **To make the side:** Whisk together the shallot, mustard, vinegar, olive oil, and salt and pepper. Toss the steamed green beans with the dressing. Top with the blue cheese and chopped walnuts. Season with salt and pepper if necessary.

8. Add the green beans to your serving plates. Slice the loin very thin, about ½-inch (13 mm) thick, and add to the serving plate. Pour the sauce over the loin and enjoy!

* Cranberry sauce or lingonberry jelly will work if you can't find red currant jelly.

GUNSLINGER BURRITOS

SERVES 2

The Dark Tower is Stephen King's epic fantasy. It follows Roland, a gunslinger, and his four companions as they quest to find the Dark Tower. The Dark Tower is basically the center point of all dimensions, the glue that holds many universes together. During the ka-tets adventures, Roland takes whatever meat and non-poisonous plants they can find and wraps them in edible leaves. Eddie refers to these as "Gunslinger Burritos." These aren't supposed to be very tasty (they're more for necessity than enjoyment), but we'll try out one of these burritos on what might have been a particularly good day.

In "The Drawing of the Three," Roland shoots a deer, which provided the ka-tet with some much-needed meat. Roland also had a salt lick, which he kept around for curing meat. Wild onions, garlic, and mushrooms are relatively easy to find and harvest when on a journey. Feel free to make any substitutions or additions you like, as Roland would use whatever the ka-tet had available at the time. Do not slice with your hands—he who slices with his hands has forgotten the face of his father . . .

INGREDIENTS

8 ounces (227 g) venison backstrap or other lean game meat, trimmed and brought to room temperature

19 pinches (1 teaspoon) salt

1 tablespoon lard or other animal fat

¼ cup (40 g) chopped wild onion or 2 green onions, chopped

1 teaspoon minced wild garlic or 1 clove regular garlic, minced

1 cup (100 g) sliced porcini or chanterelle mushrooms

2 large collard green leaves, stems removed

1. Brine the venison by coating it with the salt and set aside at room temperature for 1 hour. Then shake off the salt and pat the steaks dry with a paper towel.

2. Preheat a grill or griddle to hot, then grill the steaks for 15–20 minutes, or until medium-rare to medium. Test the steak using your fingers—if it's too soft when you poke it, it's not done; if it's hard when you poke it, it's overdone. You want just a bit of give when you poke it. When done, let the steak rest.

3. Melt the lard or other fat in a skillet over medium-high heat, then add the onions and garlic, and sauté until they soften. Add the mushrooms and cook until they are brown and juicy.

4. Now that the steak has rested, slice it into ½-inch-thick (13 mm) slices.

5. Now construct the Gunslinger Burritos. Take each collard green leaf and spread it out. Top with the sliced venison and the sautéed onions, garlic, and mushrooms. Roll up like a burrito and eat like a gunslinger!

CAKES

— AND —

CUPCAKES

LEMON CAKES

MAKES 20 CAKES

Oh, the food of *A Song of Ice and Fire*. For someone who claims not to be a great cook, George R. R. Martin sure knows how to make up some mouthwatering foodstuffs. There is an infinite amount of foods to choose from in *ASolaF*, enough to fill an entire cookbook of its own. Happily, there is one! *A Feast of Ice and Fire* would look pretty good next to this cookbook on your nerdy cookbook shelf. It's definitely on mine! As great as the official cookbook is, I had to try my hand at a few recipes myself.

One of the more memorable sweet treats in *ASolaF* is Sansa Stark's favorite pastry: Lemon Cakes. Lemon Cakes are mentioned fairly often in the books, but not described in detail. My impression of them is that they are a sort of teatime treat for young lords and ladies to enjoy. I pictured them being rustic in appearance (by modern standards; they'd be fancy in Elizabethan times and by Westerosi standards) and having a dense, moist texture with intense lemon flavor. My cakes are just that, and baked with a candied lemon slice for garnish.

INGREDIENTS

Butter or nonstick spray, for greasing

2 lemons, thinly sliced and seeded

1 cup (240 ml) water

2½ cups (500 g) granulated sugar, divided

2½ cups (280 g) flour

½ teaspoon baking powder

½ teaspoon baking soda

1 teaspoon salt

1 cup or 2 sticks (240 g) butter, softened

2 eggs

2 tablespoons lemon zest

¾ cup (180 ml) fresh lemon juice, divided

1 cup (240 ml) buttermilk

1. Preheat the oven to 350°F (180°C) and grease the muffin tin(s).

2. In a pot, boil the lemon slices in the water and 1 cup (200 g) of the sugar for about 15 minutes. Drain and set aside.

3. In a medium bowl, combine the flour, baking powder, baking soda, and salt.

4. In a large bowl, beat the butter and 1 cup (200 g) of the sugar until light and fluffy. Beat in the eggs, then stir in the lemon zest and 2 tablespoons (30 ml) of the lemon juice.

5. Beat in the dry ingredients and then the buttermilk.

6. Place 1 lemon slice in the bottom of each muffin cup and pour the batter over the slices, evenly dividing the batter among the cups.

7. Bake until the cakes are firm and golden, 15–20 minutes. Remove from the oven and let cool.

8. Mix together the remaining ⅝ cup (150 ml) lemon juice and ½ cup (100 g) sugar. Poke holes into the cakes, then slowly pour the lemon-sugar mixture over the cakes so the juice is absorbed into the cakes. Set aside for 5–10 minutes.

9. Remove the cakes from the tin(s) and serve lemon-slice side up!

DELICIOUS MOIST CAKE

SERVES 8–10

INGREDIENTS

CAKE
Butter or nonstick spray,
  for greasing
1²/₃ cups (160 g) flour, plus
  more for the pans
1 cup (125 g) unsweetened
  cocoa powder
1½ teaspoons baking soda
1 teaspoon salt
½ cup (100 g) shortening
1½ cups (300 g) sugar
2 eggs
1 teaspoon vanilla extract
1½ cups (360 g) buttermilk
½ cup (120 ml) cherry liqueur,
  or to taste

FILLING
2 × 14.5-ounce (411 g) can tart
  cherries
3 cups (700 ml) heavy
  whipping cream
¼ cup (25 g) confectioners'
  sugar
3 tablespoons cocoa powder

GARNISH
1 semisweet chocolate bar,
  frozen
8 maraschino cherries, stemmed
1 white candle

I fell in love with *Portal* a little late. I remember a friend telling me about it—something about shooting portals at walls? I didn't really get it. When I finally gave the game a shot a few years later, I spent the whole night playing through and finished it in the wee hours of the morning, and then promptly passed out. In *Portal*, you find yourself in a research facility with no idea how you got there. You are told by GLaDOS (an artificial intelligence with some emotional issues) that if you complete a series of tests, you will be given cake and grief counseling. Soon you find out that the cake is a lie.

So, the cake. The famous, ever-popular, and often-referenced cake. There is an Easter egg in the game itself where you can find a recipe for cake written in binary code, but the recipe is only an ingredients list for plain chocolate cake and lacks instructions . . . though it does have some great suggestions for garnishes. According to the developers, the design of the cake (which you do finally see at the end in most versions of the game) was inspired by a real cake from the Chinese bakery near their place of work, identified as a Black Forest cake. Black Forest cake is a kind of German cake that has chocolate, whipped cream, cherries, and a cherry-flavored liqueur called *kirschwasser*. It has four layers and is filled with boozy chocolate cherry goodness. Bake this cake and throw a big party that all your friends are invited to! Don't forget to invite your weighted companion cube . . . Oh, wait . . .

1. Preheat the oven to 350°F (180°C).
2. **To make the cake:** Grease and flour two 8-inch (20 cm) cake pans, or line them with parchment paper.
3. Combine the flour, cocoa, baking soda, and the salt in a large bowl. Set aside.
4. In a separate large bowl, beat the shortening and sugar together until fluffy. Add the eggs and vanilla, and beat thoroughly.
5. Slowly beat the dry ingredients into the wet ingredients, occasionally alternating with the buttermilk. Beat until everything is combined.
6. Pour the batter into the cake pans and bake for 35–40 minutes, or until a wooden pick comes out clean when inserted into the centers of the cakes. Let the cakes cool completely—by keeping them in the fridge for a few hours, they will be easier to cut. Meanwhile, make the filling.
7. **To make the filling:** Drain the canned cherries in a colander to remove most of the juice. Set aside.
8. Beat the whipping cream with the confectioners' sugar, until it thickens to the desired consistency. Set aside a small amount of the whipped-cream mixture for decorating the cake. Mix the cocoa powder into the remaining whipped cream mixture.
9. After the cakes have cooled, cut each cake in half horizontally to make four layers. Sprinkle each layer with the cherry liqueur.
10. Place one cake layer on the serving dish you wish to use. Spread about one-sixth of the whipped cream on the layer and one-third of the cherries on top of the whipped cream.
11. Place the second cake layer on top of the first. Spread one-sixth of the whipped cream on the second layer and one-third of the cherries on top.
12. Add the third cake layer. Spread one-sixth of the whipped cream on top along with the remaining cherries.
13. Top with the remaining cake layer. Frost the top and sides of the cake with any remaining whipped cream.
14. Use a vegetable peeler to create thin shavings from the chocolate bar. Gently pat the shavings onto the sides and top of the cake, completely coating it. Wear gloves—melting chocolate can get messy!
15. Use the reserved whipped-cream mixture to dot eight small circles around the top of the cake. Place your stemless maraschino cherries on each one.
16. Place the white candle in the center of the cake and light it. Congratulations, you have made the cake a reality!

CREME-FILLED CAKES

MAKES 8–12 CAKES

INGREDIENTS

CAKES
2 cups (250 g) cake flour
1¼ cups (250 g) sugar
1 tablespoon baking powder
1 teaspoon salt
½ cup or 1 stick (120 g) butter,
   softened
1 cup (240 ml) milk
1 teaspoon vanilla extract
2 eggs
Nonstick spray, for greasing
1 tube of ready-made white
   decorative frosting

CHOCOLATE CREME FILLING
1 jar or 7 ounces (200 g)
   marshmallow creme
⅓ cup (40 g) confectioners'
   sugar
½ cup (60 g) cocoa powder
½ cup (100 g) shortening
1 teaspoon vanilla extract
1 tablespoon evaporated milk
Pinch salt

I lack hand-eye coordination so I tend to be very bad at shooters, and because of that, it's hard for me to get into them. *Bioshock* is an exception. Developed by Irrational Games, *Bioshock* is almost universally acknowledged as an exceptional and unforgettable gaming experience. It takes place in a secret underwater city called Rapture. Rapture was built by an ambitious American shortly after the end of World War II for the purpose of forming a completely isolated capitalist society untainted by government or religion. Shockingly, this didn't exactly work out. The isolation of Rapture made it somewhat of a time capsule, but the lack of moral or governmental limitations in invention has allowed for some very advanced technology to be created, so it's a completely unique game environment.

The food is mostly of a pre-packaged variety with a focus on convenience. These Creme-Filled Cakes are one of only three kinds of food found in the game, along with potato chips and Pep Bars. There is more than twice that amount of alcohol varieties in the game, which tells you a lot about the citizens of Rapture. The cakes come in a sort of log shape, much like a certain beloved snack cake found in the real world. They also appear to be filled with chocolate creme and have sort of a squiggly frosting design on top.

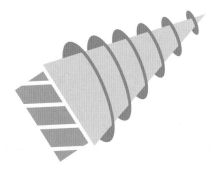

1. Preheat the oven to 350°F (180°C).

2. **To make the cakes:** If you don't have a canoe pan, I recommend making the cake molds first. Tear out a 12-inch-long (30 cm) sheet of aluminum foil. Fold it once lengthwise and then once crosswise. Place a spice jar in the center and wrap the aluminum foil around it, tucking in the ends to create a trough-like shape. Make sure the tops are open so you can pour in your batter. Remove the spice jar. Repeat until you have about 10 of these.

3. In a large mixing bowl, sift together the flour, sugar, baking powder, and salt. Add the butter, milk, and vanilla, and beat with a hand mixer for 3–4 minutes. Add the eggs and beat for 3 more minutes.

4. Spray the cake mold(s) with the nonstick spray. Evenly pour the batter among the mold(s)—they should be around three-quarters full. Depending on the size of the spice jar used, you can end up with anywhere between 8 and 12 cakes.

5. Bake the cakes for about 30 minutes, or until a toothpick inserted in the center of one comes out clean. Let the cakes cool in their cases for 10 minutes, then remove and transfer to a wire rack to cool completely. Meanwhile, make the filling.

6. **To make the chocolate creme filling:** Combine all the filling ingredients in a large bowl and beat until light and fluffy.

7. Place the filling into a pastry bag with a narrow attachment. Using a chopstick, evenly poke three holes into the bottom of one of the cakes. Sort of swish your chopstick around a bit in there to create more room for the filling. Pipe the chocolate filling into each of the holes, repeating this process for each cake.

8. When all the cakes are filled, attach a narrow frosting piper onto the tube of white decorative frosting and draw squiggles on the top of each of the cakes.

9. Stuff all the cakes into your mouth immediately while in the middle of a battle.

BUTTER CAKES

MAKES 12 CAKES

I am a huge fan of *Silent Hill* and have long lamented that it's not a great environment for noms. Being trapped in a hell dimension of guilt and torture doesn't exactly make you hungry, as Heather points out in *Silent Hill 3*. So, when I discovered the presence of the mysterious Butter Cakes, I was ecstatic. Apparently, there's a running gag among *Silent Hill* fans to try to find all the boxes. So far, Butter Cakes have been discovered in the second, third, and fourth games. I know that not a lot of people like *SH4*, but I think it has the scariest monster in any game ever—the one with the baby heads that points and whispers at you. Eeeeeeesh.

INGREDIENTS

CAKES

Butter or nonstick spray, for
  greasing
½ cup or 1 stick (120 g)
  unsalted butter, softened
1 cup (200 g) sugar
2 eggs, divided
1 teaspoon vanilla extract
1 tablespoon imitation butter
  flavor
1½ cups (180 g) cake flour
Pinch salt
2 teaspoons baking powder
¼ cup (60 ml) whole milk

GLAZE

¼ cup or ½ stick (60 g) butter
1 cup (100 g) confectioners'
  sugar
1 teaspoon imitation butter
  flavor
1 tablespoon milk
12 maraschino cherries

1. Preheat the oven to 350°F (180°C).

2. **To make the cakes:** Grease or line a muffin tin(s) with cupcake liners.

3. In a large bowl, use a mixer to cream together the butter and sugar. Add one of the eggs and continue mixing. Once the egg is incorporated, add the other egg, vanilla extract, and 1 tablespoon of the imitation butter flavor, and continue to mix for a minute or so until smooth.

4. In a separate bowl, combine the flour, salt, and baking powder.

5. Slowly mix the dry ingredients into the wet ingredients, and then slowly mix in the milk until the batter is smooth. Evenly divide the batter among the muffin tin cups.

6. Bake for 20–25 minutes, or until the edges of the cakes are golden and a toothpick inserted into the center of a cake comes out clean.

7. **To make the glaze:** Around 15 minutes before the cupcakes finish baking, make the glaze to top them. Heat the butter in a saucepan over medium heat until golden brown, about 10 minutes. Transfer the butter to a bowl. Add the confectioners' sugar, 1 teaspoon of imitation butter flavor, and milk, and stir until smooth. If the glaze is too thick, add more milk; if it is too thin, add more confectioners' sugar.

8. While the cakes are still hot, pour the glaze on top of them and insert one cherry into the center of each cake by pressing down gently so it's partially imbedded.

SWEET ROLL

MAKES 2–6 ROLLS

The highly desirable Sweet Roll is probably the most well-known food from *The Elder Scrolls* series. The stolen Sweet Roll has been a running gag in *Elder Scroll* games dating all the way back to *Arena*, where it was referenced in a theoretical question to determine your character class based on the morality of your answer. Now, Sweet Rolls are an alchemy ingredient in *Oblivion*, an actual consumable item in *Skyrim*, and even appeared in *Fallout*.

It is unknown what exactly a Sweet Roll is; what is known is that they are so tasty that people want to steal them from you—a crime punishable by a night in jail. Presumably, they are a delicious sugary baked good. In *Oblivion*, they have a shape sort of like a tall muffin or a chef's hat. In *Skyrim*, they look like a volcano with white icing. The difference in appearance may be due to regional differences in Tamriel, as *Oblivion* takes place in Cyrodill and *Skyrim* takes place in . . . Skyrim. I went with the *Skyrim* appearance. Enjoy a volcano-shaped cinnamon cake filled with sugary, buttery, nutty goodness, topped with cream-cheese icing. There are two ways to bake these: with a mini Bundt-cake pan for a perfect shape (these can be found fairly easily online) or in a standard glass measuring cup.

INGREDIENTS

CAKE

1½ cups (180 g) flour
½ cup (100 g) granulated sugar
2 teaspoons baking powder
Pinch salt
2 tablespoons ground
cinnamon
⅓ cup (80 ml) milk
1 egg
2 teaspoons vanilla extract
¼ cup or ½ stick (60 g) butter,
melted
Butter or nonstick spray, for
greasing

FILLING

¼ cup or ½ stick (60 g) butter,
softened
½ cup (30 g) chopped pecan
nuts
1 tablespoon ground cinnamon
¼ cup (60 g) packed brown
sugar

ICING

¼ cup or 2 ounces (60 g) cream
cheese, softened
1½ cups (15 0g) confectioners'
sugar
2 tablespoons milk

1. Preheat the oven to 350°F (180°C).

2. **To make the cake:** Combine the flour, sugar, baking powder, salt, and cinnamon in a large bowl.

3. Mix together the milk, egg, vanilla extract, and butter in a separate bowl.

4. Add the wet ingredients to the dry ingredients and combine thoroughly.

5. Grease the inside of an oven-safe glass measuring cup or mini Bundt-cake pan. If using a glass cup, add the batter to the 1 or 1½ cup (240 or 350 ml) line, depending on how tall you want the cake to be. If using the Bundt-cake pan, simply add an even amount of batter to each cup.

6. Bake for 25–30 minutes, or until you can stick in a knife and it comes out clean. Remove from the oven and let the cake(s) cool. Once cool, carefully remove from the measuring cup or pan so it does not break.

7. If using a glass measuring cup, the cake is going to be upside down (so the wider part is at the bottom) and may be awkwardly rounded on the bottom side. To fix this, simply cut off the rounded bottom with a knife to make it level. Set the cake down with the wider leveled side on the bottom. Use a spoon or fork to carve a hole at the top of the cake—this is where you will put the filling.

8. **To make the filling:** Mix together all the filling ingredients. Stuff the mixture into the hole(s) in the cake(s).

9. **To make the icing:** Whisk or beat together all the icing ingredients until smooth and thick. Gently drizzle the icing on top of the cake(s).

10. Serve or have the Sweet Rolls all to yourself! Remember, in Skyrim, stealing a Sweet Roll is punishable by a night in jail.

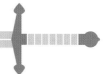

CAULDRON CAKES

MAKES 20 CAKES

Cauldron Cakes are one of the many magical treats that witches and wizards enjoy in the world of *Harry Potter*. They are purchased by an eleven-year-old Harry Potter for himself and his new friend, Ron, on their very first journey to Hogwarts on the Hogwarts Express. J. K. Rowling doesn't really explain how the cakes look or taste in the books, so readers have come up with some imaginative interpretations. For this recipe, I was inspired by the artwork on J. K. Rowling's website, Pottermore, in which they look like cute, little chocolate cakes filled with some sort of green goo to resemble a bubbling cauldron.

INGREDIENTS

CAKES

Butter or nonstick spray, for
  greasing
1 cup (120 g) flour
⅓ cup (40 g) unsweetened
  cocoa powder
1 teaspoon baking powder
1 teaspoon allspice
½ teaspoon salt
½ cup (100 g) shortening
¾ cup (150 g) sugar
1 egg
1 teaspoon vanilla extract
1 cup (240 g) buttermilk

TOPPING

1 tablespoon cornstarch
½ tablespoon water
14-ounce (396 g) can
  sweetened condensed milk
¼ cup (50 g) shortening
A few drops green food
  coloring
Flavor extract (your choice)
Pearl sprinkles
Green sugar sprinkles

1. Preheat the oven to 350°F (180°C).

2 **To make the cakes:** Grease a muffin tin(s).

3. In a medium bowl, combine the flour, cocoa powder, baking powder, allspice, and salt.

4. In a separate large bowl, beat together the shortening and sugar. Add the egg and vanilla and beat until fluffy.

5. Slowly beat the dry ingredients into the wet ingreditents, occasionally alternating with the buttermilk. Evenly divide the batter among the holes in the muffin tin(s).

6. Bake for about 20 minutes, or until a fork inserted into the center of a cake comes out clean. Let the cakes cool, then remove them from the tin(s) and transfer to a wire rack to cool completely. Meanwhile, make the topping.

7. **To make the topping:** Combine the cornstarch and water to form a paste.

8. Beat together the remaining topping ingredients—except the sprinkles—including the cornstarch paste you just made. The finished texture should be like a thick and gooey slime. If it's too runny, add more shortening; if it's too thick (like frosting), add more sweetened condensed milk.

9. Take the cooled cakes and carve out a shallow hole on the bottom side of each one to be the inside of the cauldron that holds the goo.

10. Spoon the goo into the holes so that they are almost overflowing, then top with the sprinkles.

11. Accio Cauldron Cakes!

CAKE BLOCK

SERVES 6-10

INGREDIENTS

1 cup or 2 sticks (240 g) butter, softened
2 cups (450 g) white sugar
4 eggs
1 tablespoon vanilla extract
3 cups (360 g) cake flour
1 tablespoon baking powder
¾ cup (180 ml) whole milk
1 teaspoon salt
Butter or nonstick spray, for greasing
1½ cups (485 g) strawberry jelly
White fondant
Red fondant (recommended) or red food coloring

Minecraft is an award-winning indie game that reached an unfathomable level of popularity in a relatively short amount of time. In the game, you mine and craft materials in order to build yourself a shelter and survive, or you run around punching things and get beaten to death by zombies and/or die of starvation—like me. One of the best things about *Minecraft* is that you are given absolute freedom to build whatever you want, however you want. This freedom has allowed players to make some very elaborate worlds and buildings, especially in the game's creative mode. Everything in the game— from the animals to the clouds—is rendered as textured blocks, including the cake.

Most of the prepared food in *Minecraft* is only shown in your inventory, but the cake is an exception. The Cake Block is made by combining three buckets of milk, two units of sugar, three units of wheat, and one egg. When the cake is crafted, it needs to be placed on top of another block in order to be enjoyed. Each slice of cake recovers two hunger units, and eating the entire cake will recover twelve hunger units. Unlike the other foods in *Minecraft*, slices of cake are eaten instantaneously and you can gobble down the whole cake in seconds—much like real life. The cake is depicted as having white icing and little red pixels on top.

This recipe is for my favorite white cake layered with strawberry jam filling to complement the red pixels. You will need to use fondant to recreate the geometric patterns and clean lines of the cake's topping.

1. Preheat the oven to 350°F (180°C).

2. In a large bowl, cream together the butter and sugar, then add the eggs and vanilla extract, and continue mixing.

3. Mix in the flour, baking powder, and salt.

4. Grease two 8 x 8-inch (20 x 20 cm) baking pans and divide the batter equally between them.

5. Bake for 30-40 minutes, or until a fork inserted into the center of each cake comes out clean. Remove from the oven and leave to cool.

6. Once cool, carefully level the tops of the cakes using a sharp knife.

7. Set one cake on a board and spoon half the jelly on top, spreading it around evenly, keeping it about 1 inch (2.5 cm) in from the outer edges of the cake. Set the other cake on top and spread the rest of the jelly over the top and slightly over the edge of the second cake layer.

8. Here comes the hard part: fondant is unforgiving and difficult to work with, but I'll do my best to explain this next step. Roll out the white fondant until you have a surface area large enough to cover your entire cake.

9. Carefully lift the fondant sheet by gently flipping one end over the rolling pin and raising it up and onto the top of the cake, making sure the cake is completely covered. Then, using your hands, gently press the fondant around the cake, trying to avoid making any folds or creases.

10. Using a sharp knife, scalpel, or scissors, cut out the square pattern in the fondant on the sides of the cake. I highly recommend creating a template or stencil by cutting the shape out of some cardboard before attempting this, along with using a photo for reference.

11. You have a few options for the red squares on the top of the cake. Option 1: Roll out some pre-made red fondant and cut out the square shapes. Wet them lightly on the back and arrange them on top of the cake. This is the easiest and best-looking option. Option 2: Roll out the white fondant, cut out the square shapes, and individually paint them with red food coloring. Then lightly wet the back (unpainted) side of each square and carefully arrange them on top of the cake. Option 3: Position the white fondant squares and paint them in situ with red food coloring.

12. Cut the cake into 6 (or more) square slices and enjoy!

1UP MUSHROOM CUPCAKES

MAKES 12 CUPCAKES

INGREDIENTS

CAKES

Butter or nonstick spray, for greasing
½ cup or 1 stick (120 g) butter, softened
1 cup (225 g) sugar
2 eggs, divided
1 teaspoon vanilla extract
1⅓ cups (180 g) cake flour
Pinch salt
1 teaspoon baking powder
¼ cup (60 ml) whole milk

FROSTING

½ cup or 1 stick (120 g) butter, softened
½ cup (112 g) shortening
2 cups (200 g) confectioners' sugar
½ tablespoon milk
Green or red food coloring
2 teaspoons imitation butter flavoring
White chocolate buttons, white modeling chocolate, or white fondant, for decorating

Like most people born after 1985, I grew up playing *Super Mario Bros.* games. The series, created by Nintendo's very own mad genius Shigeru Miyamoto, is one of the most widely known and beloved game series of all time. The games feature Mario, a portly Italian plumber with inexplicably superior athletic ability and stamina. He is in love with Princess Toadstool, aka Peach. Unfortunately for Mario, the princess is kidnapped by King Koopa, aka Bowser, about every year or so. Fun fact: Mario actually made his first appearance as Jumpman in Nintendo's 1981 arcade game *Donkey Kong*.

One of the many iconic items in the Mario series is the 1Up Mushroom. Unlike the red toadstool, which allows Mario to grow in size, the 1Up Mushroom gives Mario another life and another chance to fall into the abyss or be killed by fire-breathing plants. The 1Up's appearance has changed over the years, but most will recognize it as the bright green toadstool with white spots. I generally try to avoid making cakes that look like things that are not supposed to be cakes, but this is an exception. Mario was the catalyst that made gaming what it is today and is a piece of geek cultural history. Short of encouraging people to eat a raw toadstool (do NOT eat raw toadstools . . .), there wasn't any other way to pay tribute to Mario in food.

You can make the frosting in this one either green or red, depending on whether you want another life or to grow in size. Well, eat too many of these babies and you'll grow in size either way.

1. Preheat the oven to 350°F (180°C).

2. **To make the cakes:** Grease or line a muffin tin(s) with cupcake liners.

3. In a large bowl, cream together the butter and sugar. Add one of the eggs and continue mixing. Once the first egg is fully incorporated, add the other egg and the vanilla extract and continue to mix for a minute or so until smooth.

4. In a separate bowl, sift together the flour, salt, and baking powder.

5. Slowly mix the dry ingredients into the wet ingredients, then slowly mix in the milk until the batter is smooth.

6. Divide the batter evenly among the muffin-tin cups until each is three-quarters full.

7. Bake for 20–25 minutes, or until the edges of the cakes are golden and a toothpick inserted in the center of a cake comes out clean.

8. **To make the frosting:** Cream together the butter and shortening. Whip the confectioners' sugar into the butter and shortening, then add the milk, green or red food coloring, and imitation butter flavor, and continue to whip until you get the preferred consistency and color. The frosting should be spreadable but stiff. If it's too runny, add more confectioners' sugar; if it's too stiff, add more milk.

9. Spread the green or red frosting on top of the cupcakes and decorate with white dots.

CREAM CHEESE FROSTED GORAPPLE CAKE

SERVES 8–10

After dedicating years to *World of Warcraft*, *Guild Wars 2*, and even this really obscure Korean MMO called *ROSE Online*, I told myself I would never, ever play another MMO. . . . But then Bethesda went and had an *ESO* sale. And I'm a sucker for an *Elder Scrolls* game. Unfortunately for my productivity, *ESO* is just like any other *Elder Scrolls* game, with gorgeous scenery, interesting lore, fun gameplay, and a lot of detail. Yep, just like every other *Elder Scrolls* game . . . except there's no real ending and you can just keep playing it indefinitely. Bye-bye, social life! See ya later, hopes and dreams!

There are lots of intriguing foods in *ESO*. I chose this recipe because I owe it a debt for getting me from level 35 to level 40 with minimal death and wasted soul gems. And it just sounds really tasty. Honestly, though, *The Elder Scrolls* series has been coming through with tasty-sounding foods for years. The in-game recipe just includes carrot, apple, and flour, so we're going to embellish it a bit to make this work.

CAKE

¾ cup or 1½ sticks (180 g)
  unsalted butter, softened
¾ cup (150 g) granulated sugar
¼ cup (60 g) packed light
  brown sugar
2 large eggs
1 cup (125 g) all-purpose flour
Sweet Spice Blend (page 12),
  to taste
½ teaspoon baking powder
¼ teaspoon baking soda
Pinch salt
2 carrots, peeled and finely
  shredded
2 apples (any kind) peeled,
  cored, and shredded

FROSTING

3 ounces (85 g) cream cheese,
  softened
1¼ cups (155 g) confectioner's
  sugar
1 tablespoon unsalted butter,
  softened
1 teaspoon lemon juice
¼ teaspoon vanilla extract
Red and orange gel food
  coloring

1. Preheat the oven to 350°F (180°C).

2. **To make the cake:** Grease a 9-inch (23 cm) baking pan.

3. In a large bowl, cream together the butter and sugars. Add the eggs and beat for another minute until incorporated and fluffy.

4. Combine the flour, spices, baking powder, baking soda, and salt. Gradually add the dry ingredients to the wet ingredients just until combined. Stir in the shredded carrot and apple. Spoon the batter into the prepared baking pan.

5. Bake for 25–30 minutes, or until a toothpick inserted in the center of the cake comes out clean. Let the cake cool and set before removing it from the pan for frosting. After the cake is almost completely cool, prepare the frosting.

6. **To make the frosting:** In a medium bowl, combine all the frosting ingredients and beat until smooth. If necessary, keep adding the food coloring at a 2:1 red-to-orange ratio for the frosting to achieve the same burnt orange color as in the game. Spread over the cake with an icing spatula or frosting tool.

MARCHPANE CAKE

SERVES 8-10

His Dark Materials is a fantasy trilogy written by Philip Pullman. Reading *His Dark Materials* was, for me, very similar to reading *Peter Pan*, in that it's certainly *about* children but it doesn't seem like it's necessarily *for* children. The story follows a young girl named Lyra, who lives in an alternate universe where people's souls are entities in the form of animals that follow their owners around. The series goes to very unexpected places, and although it has very strong fantasy elements, the overall story is a lot more like *Paradise Lost* than *The Lord of the Rings*.

Oddly enough, although *His Dark Materials* (mostly) takes place in an alternate universe, the food is based in reality. There's chocolatl, which is chocolate; Kendal Mint Cakes, which are energy bars used by mountaineers; and blubber, which is, well, marine animal fat. There was one food that stood out to me, and that is the Marchpane (or Marzipan) Cake, which appears in the third book of the trilogy, *The Amber Spyglass*. I am aware that Marzipan cakes are definitely a real thing, but this one was fairly special. Enjoy it with a nice cup of chocolatl; it tastes almost like falling in love . . .

INGREDIENTS

1 Yellow Cake Mix (page 14)
1 tablespoon lemon zest
6 ounces (175 g) almond paste
1½ cups (180 g) almond flour
1½ cups (185 g) confectioners'
  sugar, plus extra for dusting
2 teaspoons almond extract
1 teaspoon rose water
1 egg white
Warmed apricot jelly, for
  glazing

1. Prepare the yellow cake mix, but in step 2 of that recipe, beat in the lemon zest and almond paste with the butter and sugar. Let the cake cool while you prepare the marzipan.

2. Place the almond flour and confectioners' sugar in a food processor, and pulse until combined, making sure you break up any lumps. Add the almond extract and rose water to the food processor, and pulse to combine, then add the egg white and process until a thick dough is formed.

3. Dust your work surface with confectioners' sugar, then turn out the almond marzipan dough and knead it a few times.

4. Roll out the marzipan as evenly as possible until it's large enough to cover the cake.

5. Use a clean glazing brush to spread the warmed apricot jelly onto the marzipan. Use your rolling pin to carefully lift the marzipan up and onto the cake, jelly side down. Use your hands to gently press the marzipan onto the cake. The jelly should help with this, acting like glue. Usually it's best to smooth the top first, then the sides. If you notice air bubbles or pleating making things uneven, just slightly lift the marzipan to let the air escape or to unfold the pleat. When the marzipan is smoothly covering the cake, trim the excess from the bottom. Decorate the cake however you like!

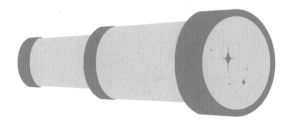

SEED CAKES

MAKES 12 SMALL CAKES OR 4-5 RAMEKIN CAKES

The Hobbit was Tolkien's precursor to *The Lord of the Rings* trilogy, which is widely accepted as the "grandfather" of high fantasy. Without *The Hobbit*'s success, there may never have been *The Lord of the Rings*, which in turn inspired countless other authors to create their own works of fantasy. Without *The Hobbit* and *The Lord of the Rings*, we may never have had phenomena like *Harry Potter* or *Game of Thrones*, or even *Dungeons and Dragons*. Personally, I wouldn't want to live in such a world.

In the beginning of the classic tale, Bilbo very unexpectedly finds his home full of hungry dwarves, and Balin specifically requests Seed Cakes. Like any respectable Hobbit, Bilbo already had some cakes prepared and is able to serve up these tasty morsels, along with an assortment of other delicious foods, to all thirteen dwarves.

INGREDIENTS

CAKES
1 Yellow Cake Mix (page 14)
⅛ cup (20 g) caraway seeds
½ cup (70 g) poppy seeds, plus
  extra for topping
Zest of 1 orange (approximately
  1 tablespoon)

GLAZE
1½ cups (185 g) confectioners'
  sugar
¼ cup (60 ml) orange juice,
  plus more if necessary
1 tablespoon melted butter
½ teaspoon almond extract
1 teaspoon vanilla extract

1. **To make the cakes:** Prepare the yellow cake mix, adding all the seeds and orange zest along with the other dry ingredients in step 4 of that recipe. I recommend using ramekins or a muffin tin for baking these cakes.

2. Once the cakes have cooled, carefully remove them from their tins or ramekins.

3. **To make the glaze:** Add the confectioners' sugar to a bowl, then add in the juice, butter, and almond and vanilla extracts. Stir until it forms a smooth glaze. Add more orange juice if it's too thick.

4. Carefully pour the glaze onto the top of each cake and allow it to spread naturally.

5. Once the glaze has spread a bit, sprinkle additional poppy seeds on the tops of the cakes.

DAUNTLESS CHOCOLATE CAKE

SERVES 8-10

The *Divergent* series is a trilogy of YA dystopian novels, written by Veronica Roth, set in post-apocalyptic Chicago, in a time when society is split into five factions, which each exemplify a set of personality traits. The story follows Beatrice "Tris" Prior as she comes of age and must decide which faction she belongs in. She chooses the Dauntless faction, who value fearlessness and cool tattoos. Although later she discovers she is Divergent, which means she possesses qualities from more than one faction . . . but that's beside the point, and the point is cake.

The Dauntless faction is known for things like wearing black leather, jumping off buildings, and their delicious chocolate cake. This cake is referenced frequently in the series, and always positively. But be warned, this dessert isn't for pansycakes; it's rich, decadent, and with the secret ingredient—hot coffee—it'll get you juiced up for some extreme parkour.

INGREDIENTS

CAKE
1¾ cups (215 g) all-purpose flour, plus extra for dusting
2 cups (400 g) granulated sugar
¾ cup (78 g) unsweetened cocoa powder
1½ teaspoons baking powder
1½ teaspoons baking soda
Pinch salt
2 eggs
1 cup (240 ml) whole milk
½ cup (120 ml) vegetable oil
2 teaspoons vanilla extract
1 cup (235 ml) hot coffee

FROSTING
½ cup or 1 stick (120 g) unsalted butter, softened
1½ cups (165 g) unsweetened cocoa powder
1/3 cup (80 ml) whole milk, plus a little extra
1 teaspoon vanilla extract
2½ cups (310 g) confectioners' sugar
Your favorite decorations, for topping

1. Preheat the oven to 350°F (180°C).

2. **To make the cake:** Grease and sprinkle flour onto the bottom of two 9-inch (23 cm) cake pans. In a medium bowl, stir together the flour, sugar, cocoa powder, baking powder, baking soda, and salt.

3. In a separate bowl, mix the eggs, milk, oil, and vanilla with a hand mixer.

4. Add the wet ingredients to the dry ingredients and mix for 3 minutes with the mixer. Stir in the hot coffee with a wooden spoon.

5. Pour the batter evenly into the two cake pans. Bake for 30–35 minutes, or until a toothpick inserted in the centers of the cakes comes out clean. Cool for 20 minutes before removing from the pans to cool completely. Just before the cakes are completely cool, begin the frosting.

6. **To make the frosting:** In a large bowl, beat the butter and cocoa powder together. Add the ⅓ cup (80 ml) of milk and vanilla, and beat until smooth. Gradually beat in the confectioners' sugar until the desired consistency is achieved.

7. Line your cake board or serving piece with parchment paper and carefully place one of the cakes down onto it. If your cake has a rounded top, trim this off with a sharp knife so it's flat and place this side down. Using a frosting spatula or a knife, spread the frosting evenly on top of the bottom cake layer.

8. Take the second cake (again, if it's rounded on top, trim off the rounded part) and gently place it, trimmed side down, on the frosted layer. Take about a ½ cup (100 g) of frosting and thin it out with a little milk so it spreads a little easier. Spread a thin frosting layer on the top and sides of the cake, then chill until set, about 15 minutes. If you can still see any cake, repeat this step.

9. Now, frost the cake with the regular, unthinned frosting. Start with the top of the cake, spreading the frosting all the way to the edges of the top layer. Then, frost the sides. If you have a turntable, you can spin it around as you frost for a more even coating. When you're done, remove the parchment paper. Place any decorations on the cake that you wish.

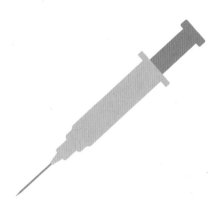

HONEYCAKES

SERVES 10-12

The Wheel of Time series, initially written by the late Robert Jordan and completed by Brandon Sanderson, is one of the greatest epic fantasies of all time. But the real question is, how's the food?

Honeycakes are one of the first foods mentioned in *The Eye of the World*, the first book of the series. Before fate fell upon Rand and his companions, they were mostly concerned with sheepherder things—like girls and Mistress al'Vere's honeycakes. Although not as important as stopping Shai'tan's evil plans, these cakes definitely deserve some attention. These treats are heavenly—the honey syrup soaks into the cake and oozes with every bite, and they pair well with spiced wine and fresh fruits . . . but perhaps avoid peaches?

INGREDIENTS

CAKES
2 large eggs
⅔ cup (230 g) orange blossom
  honey
1 teaspoon vanilla extract
1½ cups (185 g) all-purpose
  flour
Sweet Spice Blend (page 12),
  to taste
1 tablespoon orange zest
2 teaspoons baking powder
Pinch baking soda
1 teaspoon salt
1 cup (120 g) heavy whipping
  cream

HONEY SYRUP
1 cup (350 g) honey
½ cup (100 g) granulated sugar
¾ cup (180 ml) water
1 teaspoon lemon juice

1. Preheat the oven to 325°F (170°C) and grease 6 ramekins or individual cake pans or a muffin tin(s).

2. **To make the cakes:** Beat the eggs in a bowl until foamy and thick, then add the honey and vanilla. Mix well.

3. In a separate bowl, sift together the flour, spice blend, zest, baking powder, baking soda, and salt.

4. Add one-third of the dry ingredients, followed by one-third of the cream, to the egg mixture. Mix well and repeat until everything is combined. Pour the batter evenly into the ramekins, cake pans, or muffin tin(s).

5. Bake for 20–30 minutes, or until a toothpick inserted in the center comes out clean. Let cool. Meanwhile, make the honey syrup.

6. **To make the honey syrup:** In a saucepan, combine the honey, sugar, and water. Bring to a simmer for around 5 minutes. Stir in the lemon juice, bring to a boil and boil for a couple minutes more.

7. Poke the cakes multiple times with toothpicks. Pour the honey syrup over the cakes and allow it to soak in for a few minutes before serving.

OTHER
DESSERTS

TURKISH DELIGHT

MAKES 26–36 PIECES

Turkish Delight isn't fictional at all, but it's such a staple of fantasy food I couldn't not make a recipe—that would pretty much be nerd blasphemy. Those who have read *The Lion, The Witch and the Wardrobe* will remember the very tense moment when little Edmund meets the sinister White Queen and stupidly reveals the location of his siblings for a bit of Turkish Delight. Edmund was kind of a jerk at that early point in the story, but the way Turkish Delight was described in the book made it seem like such a heavenly treat that you could almost—almost—empathize with the little brat.

So, Turkish Delight is actually a sweet and chewy confection that is traditionally flavored with rose water and nuts and served with a coating of confectioners' sugar. I've kept this recipe very old school because why mess with tradition when it's already so good you'll sell out your own brothers and sisters for a piece?

INGREDIENTS

Oil, for greasing
1 cup (240 ml) water
2 tablespoons gelatin
1¾ cups (150 g) sugar
¼ teaspoon citric acid
½ cup (50 g) pistachios, shelled
  and chopped
1 teaspoon vanilla extract
2 teaspoons rose water or
  other flavoring extract
  of your choice
¼ cup (25 g) confectioners'
  sugar
2 tablespoons cornstarch
Few drops food coloring
  (optional)

1. Grease a 6 × 6-inch (15 × 15 cm) baking pan.

2. Place the water in a large saucepan and sprinkle over the gelatin. Set aside until the gelatin is a little springy.

3. Add the sugar and citric acid to the gelatin water, place the pan over a gentle heat, and stir constantly until dissolved. Bring the mixture to a boil. Boil for 15 minutes without stirring. Remove from the heat and set aside for 10 minutes.

4. Stir in the vanilla extract, rose water, pistachios, and a few drops of food coloring (if using).

5. Pour into the prepared pan. Leave uncovered in a cool place for 24 hours.

6. Sift the confectioners' sugar and cornstarch together onto a sheet of parchment paper. Turn out the set Turkish Delight onto the paper and cut into squares using a sharp knife.

7. Toss pieces in the confectioners' sugar-cornstarch mixture so that all sides are coated. Pack the squares into airtight containers lined with parchment paper and dust with the remaining confectioners' sugar-cornstarch mixture.

AIR NOMAD'S FRUIT PIES

MAKES 1 PIE

It's impossible to resist a series with so many good food moments. For some context, the people of Avatar fall into four different nations that are each devoted to one of the four elements: earth, air, fire, and water. Some people in these nations have command of their national element; this skill is known as bending. The national element and the bending skill has a lot of influence on the culture of the nation and, of course, their cuisine. The fire nation tends to like things spicy, the water tribe eats a lot of seafood and soups, etc. These fruit pies are an airbender dessert that appeared in the third episode of the series in a flashback/memory of Avatar Ang's, in which he fondly remembers his airbending master making the pies so that they could airbend them onto the heads of the other air monks. Ang's master tells him that the secret is in the "gooey center." In a later episode, Ang divulges that the pies are his favorite food!

My idea for this recipe was to make a delicious coconut frangipane pie tart with a gooey jelly center. It's topped with colorful lime-flavored whipped cream, which will require you to do some real airbending!

INGREDIENTS

CRUST
1¾ cups (210 g) flour, plus extra
    for dusting
¾ cup or 1½ sticks (180 g)
    butter, chilled and cubed
¼ cup (50 g) granulated sugar
2 egg yolks
1 tablespoon orange zest

FILLING
½ cup or 1 stick (120 g) butter,
    softened
½ cup (100 g) granulated sugar
2 medium eggs, beaten
¾ cup (85 g) almond meal
2 teaspoons coconut extract
1 teaspoon cornstarch
Pinch salt
3 cups (240 g) jelly or jam (I
    suggest mango, passion fruit,
    or pineapple flavored)

TOPPING
1 cup (240 ml) heavy whipping
    cream
½ cup (50 g) confectioners'
    sugar
Zest of 1 lime
Few drops food coloring color
    of your choice

1. **To make the crust:** Blend the flour and butter in a food processor until crumbly. Add the sugar and blend again briefly to combine. Add the egg yolks and orange zest, and pulse until it comes together. You may need to add a little bit of water if it seems dry.

2. Wrap the pastry in plastic wrap and chill for about 30 minutes.

3. Preheat the oven to 375°F (190°C). While the oven is preheating, make the filling.

4. **To make the filling:** Cream together the butter and sugar until smooth. Add the almond meal and blend well. Add the eggs and stir until thoroughly combined, then stir in the extract, cornstarch, and salt.

5. After the dough has chilled, flour a work surface and roll out the dought to fit a 9-inch (23 cm) pie pan. Place the dough in the pan and carefully and evenly press it onto the bottom and sides. Trim any excess dough and discard.

6. Spoon the jelly or jam onto the bottom of the pie and spread evenly. Spoon the filling on top of the jelly or jam and spread evenly, completely covering the jam.

7. Bake for 30 minutes, or until the center is firm but springy to the touch. Let cool.

8. **To make the topping:** Add all the topping ingredients into a large bowl and whip together with a mixer until peaks start to form. Be careful not to whip too much and make butter. Cover the bowl with plastic wrap and place in the refrigerator until ready to use.

9. When the pie has cooled, use a piping bag with a large star attachment to pipe the whipped cream topping onto the center of the pie in a swirling motion.

10. Airbend the pie onto someone's head.

PUMPKIN PASTIES

MAKES 12 PASTIES

INGREDIENTS

CRUST
3½ cups (420 g) flour
Pinch salt
5 teaspoons sugar
¾ cup or 1½ sticks (180 g) butter, cubed
½ cup (100 g) shortening
1 cup (240 ml) ice water, divided

FILLING
2 tablespoons unsalted butter, melted, plus extra for greasing and the pasty crusts (optional)
2 eggs, beaten
1 cup (100 g) sugar
15-ounce (425 g) can pure pumpkin
½ teaspoon salt
2 teaspoons ground cinnamon, plus extra for the pasty crusts (optional)
1 teaspoon ground ginger
1 teaspoon ground cloves
1 teaspoon ground cardamom
1 teaspoon allspice
12-ounce (354 ml) can evaporated milk

Another mouthwatering *Harry Potter* classic! Pumpkin Pasties are mentioned fairly often in the *Harry Potter* series, though they are never described in detail. They are sold at the Honeyduke's Trolley on the Hogwarts Express. They were one of the first wizard foods Harry Potter ever ate, along with Chocolate Frogs and Cauldron Cakes.

A pasty is a sort of hand pie, thought to have originated in Cornwall, England, where they are the regional specialty. They are semicircular in shape and are traditionally made with pie crust filled with meat, potatoes, and other savories. However, because in *Harry Potter* Pumpkin Pasties are sold alongside other sweets, there is a consensus that they are a dessert. I've made a simple pastry crust filled with spiced, sweetened, gooey pumpkin goodness. It's sort of like a delicious, portable pocket of pumpkin pie!

1. **To make the crust:** Combine the flour, salt, and sugar until well blended. Add the butter cubes and toss until coated. Using your hands, rub the butter into the flour until dough is in bean-size pieces.

2. Add the shortening to the dough and toss, then rub the shortening into the flour using the same method as with the butter, until you have pea-size pieces.

3. Sprinkle in about half the ice water and use your hands to squeeze the dough together, being careful not to overwork it. Keep adding a little bit of ice water at a time until the dough comes together but is not wet—you may not need to use all of the water.

4. Form the dough into a ball, cover with plastic wrap, and put in the fridge for at least 30 minutes. Meanwhile, make the filling.

5. **To make the filling:** Preheat the oven to 425°F (220°C) and grease a large casserole dish.

6. Add the eggs and sugar to a mixing bowl, and combine until well blended. Stir in the pumpkin, butter, salt, and spices. Pour in the evaporated milk and stir well.

7. Transfer the filling to the prepared dish and bake for 15 minutes. Reduce the oven temperature to 350°F (180°C) and continue baking for 45 minutes, or until your fork comes out clean when inserted into the filling. Let it cool completely. Do not turn off the oven.

8. Roll out the pastry until thin and cut into circles about 4 inches (10 cm) in diameter.

9. Put a heaping spoonful of the pumpkin mixture toward one side of the center of the circle. Fold over the crust into a semicircle and firmly press the edges closed. Cut 3 small slits in the top for venting and place on a greased cookie sheet. Repeat this step to form all the pasties.

10. Increase the oven temperature to 400°F (200°C) and bake until the crusts are a light golden brown, around 10 minutes.

11. If desired, mix some cinnamon and melted butter together and brush the pasties after they come out of the oven.

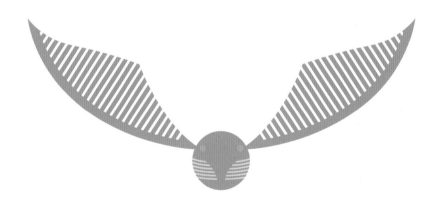

TREACLE TARTS

MAKES 12 TARTS

Harry Potter's favorite dessert! Harry loves Treacle Tarts so much that he smells them even when in the presence of Amortentia.

Treacle Tarts are a traditional English dessert, popular among children and made with golden syrup. Golden syrup has an irresistible nutty and buttery flavor, with almost the same consistency as honey. I can see why Harry likes it. It's truly liquid gold and my new favorite thing ever. Watch out, Felix Felicis! Well, pop the stuff in a flaky tart crust and it is pure heaven. And by "heaven" I mean Hogwarts.

INGREDIENTS

CRUST
1¾ cups (210 g) flour, plus extra
  for dusting
¾ cup or 1½ sticks (180 g)
  butter, chilled and diced
¼ cup (50 g) sugar
2 egg yolks
1 tablespoon orange zest

FILLING
1 cup (350 g) golden syrup
1 tablespoon molasses
2 tablespoons butter
Pinch salt
6 tablespoons bread crumbs
3 tablespoons heavy cream
1 tablespoon flour
1 tablespoon lemon zest
1 egg, beaten

Whipped cream, clotted
  cream, or vanilla ice cream,
  for serving

1. **To make the crust:** Blend the flour and butter in a food processor until crumbly. Add the sugar and briefly blend again to combine.

2. Add the egg yolks and the orange zest and pulse until it comes together. You may need to add a little bit of water if it seems dry.

3. Wrap the pastry in plastic wrap and chill for about 30 minutes.

4. Preheat the oven to 375°F (190°C). Meanwhile, make the filling.

5. **To make the filling:** Heat the golden syrup and molasses in a saucepan over medium heat for 3–5 minutes, or until loosened, stirring occasionally. Remove the syrup from the heat and stir in the butter, salt, bread crumbs, cream, flour, and zest until combined. Stir in the beaten egg and set aside.

6. Roll out the pastry on a floured surface until it is ⅛ inch (3 mm) thick, then stamp or cut out circles big enough to fit your tart tins. You can use a cookie cutter for this, if necessary.

7. Mold the circular dough cut-outs onto the bottoms and sides of the tart tins, fill each with the treacle filling, and bake for approximately 20 minutes, or until the treacle is firm and set and the crust is golden.

8. Serve hot or cold, topped with whipped cream, clotted cream, or vanilla ice cream, if desired!

SEA-SALT ICE CREAM

MAKES 2 QUARTS OR 4 PINTS

Kingdom Hearts is where *Final Fantasy* and Disney collide. In the first game, you play as Sora, a kid from an isolated island who finds himself thrown into a crazy adventure involving Disney and *Final Fantasy* characters alike. In the beginning of the second game, however, you are another kid, named Roxas. Roxas and his friends live in a place called Twilight Town and spend their time getting into trouble and eating Sea-Salt Ice Cream on top of the clock tower overlooking the town. Later in the game, the characters of *Kingdom Hearts II* can often be seen talking about—and eating—this delicious salty-sweet dessert.

Apparently, *Kingdom Hearts II* director Tetsuya Nomura had this ice cream on a trip to the Tokyo Disneyland Resort and liked it so much, he decided to work with Disney to put it into the games. It has a characteristic sky-blue color and is only ever seen being eaten on a Popsicle stick. I have learned a lot since I originally posted the recipe for Sea-Salt Ice Cream on my blog, so I have revised the original recipe and I think it is greatly improved. The ice cream is sweet, cold, smooth, and creamy with a hint of sea salt to finish. Enjoy this with your best buddies at twilight on a warm summer day.

INGREDIENTS

5 cups (1.2 L) heavy cream
2½ cups (600 ml) whole milk
1 teaspoon vanilla extract
1½ cups (300 g) sugar, divided
Sea salt, to taste
12 large egg yolks
Blue food coloring
Nonstick spray (optional)
Popsicle sticks (optional)

1. Simmer the cream, milk, vanilla extract, and 1 cup (200 g) of the sugar in a large pot, stirring with a wooden spoon, for about 15 minutes.

2. Stir the sea salt into the cream mixture in extremely tiny amounts and taste as you go. Keep adding until you get a subtle salty aftertaste.

3. Combine the egg yolks in a large bowl and lightly whisk them. Slowly add the remaining ½ cup (100 g) sugar and continue to whisk until the sugar is completely dissolved and the eggs are thick and pale yellow.

4. Gradually whisk in about 4 cups (950 ml) of the hot cream mixture. Once the hot cream is evenly whisked into the egg yolks, pour it all back into the pot with the rest of the cream. Reduce the heat to medium-low.

5. Add a few drops of the blue food coloring, a little at a time, and stir constantly until the color is right and the custard thickens, about 12 minutes. Make sure not to boil.

6. Chill the ice-cream base in the refrigerator until cold.

7. If using an ice-cream maker, transfer the chilled ice-cream base to your machine and churn according to the manufacturer's instructions—it should come out like soft serve. Spoon it into a freezer-proof container and place in the freezer until ready to serve.

8. If not using an ice-cream maker, place the chilled ice-cream base in a frozen stainless-steel bowl and let the mixture sit until the edges start to freeze, 15–20 minutes. Use a spatula or whisk to rapidly stir the ice cream, mixing in the frozen edges. Return the stainless-steel bowl to the freezer. Vigorously stir the ice cream every 30 minutes until it is firm, between 4–6 times. If it's too hard to stir, place in the fridge until it softens, then stir again.

9. If you're making Popsicles, spray the insides of the molds with nonstick spray and pour the ice cream into each mold. Add the sticks and freeze for at least 4 hours.

POFFINS

MAKES 24 POFFINS

Pokémon is a worldwide phenomenon. The video games and anime TV series blew up in a big way in the '90s, and the brand has, ahem, evolved over time. Now there are movies, card games, collectibles, and even knockoffs based on the beloved Japanese animal things. Amazingly, the brand is just as popular today as it was over a decade ago, if not even more so. On planet Earth today, approximately zero humans are unaware of the existence of Pikachu. I'm old enough to remember the world before Pokémon and let me tell you, it was about 25 percent less adorable.

As most know, the basic premise of Pokémon is that there are these creatures and you must collect them all *because reasons*. Well, sometimes your Pokémon need to eat. One of the more interesting consumables, Poffins, are depicted as little multicolored football-shaped pastries. When a Pokémon eats a Poffin, one of their conditions (smart, cute, tough, etc.) improves based on what kind of berry is used in the creation of the Poffin. I tried a few different things for Poffins, including filling them with jelly and trying to incorporate fruit in the dough itself, but let's just say it wasn't very effective. See what I did there? Their final incarnation, which I have included here, is as a light buttery roll filled with a fruity custard.

INGREDIENTS

FILLING
2 cups (475 ml) milk
¾ cup (150 g) sugar
1 teaspoon vanilla extract
Pinch salt
5 tablespoons cornstarch
6 egg yolks
1 cup (150 g) berries
   of your choice

DOUGH
1 cup (240 ml) water at 110°F
   (40°C)
2 packets (¼ oz, or 7g) active
   dry yeast
½ cup or 1 stick (120 g) butter,
   melted
¾ cup (150 g) sugar
3 eggs, plus 1 beaten egg for
   washing
Food coloring of your choice
1 teaspoon salt
4½ cups (540 g) flour, plus
   extra for dusting
White sesame seeds,
   for sprinkling

1. **To make the filling:** In a medium saucepan, bring the milk, sugar, vanilla extract, salt, cornstarch, and egg yolks to a boil, whisking constantly. Slightly reduce the heat and continue to boil for a couple minutes. Stir constantly and make sure to scrape into the corners of the saucepan.

2. Take the saucepan off the heat and plunge it into an ice-water bath to stop the eggs from cooking further. Set aside to cool completely. Meanwhile, make the dough.

3. **To make the dough:** Combine the water and yeast in a mixing bowl and let stand for 5 minutes.

4. Stir in the butter, sugar, 3 whole eggs, food coloring, and salt. Beat in the flour, 1 cup (120 g) at a time.

5. Cover the dough with plastic wrap and refrigerate for at least 2 hours.

6. Preheat the oven to 375°F (190°C) and line a baking pan with parchment paper.

7. Turn out the dough onto a floured surface and divide it into 24 pieces. Roll each piece into a ball shape.

8. Add the berries to the custard filling and them stir in. If you are using larger berries or fruit, such as strawberries, cut them into smaller pieces first.

9. Take one ball of dough at a time and press down on it to flatten slightly.

10. Spoon about 1½ teaspoons of the custard filling into the center of each slightly flattened dough ball. Pull up the sides of the dough and fold them over the filling, making sure each ball is completely sealed. You may need to wet your fingers to create a good seal. Mold each ball into the Poffin shape.

11. Let the Poffins rest somewhere warm for 25–30 minutes.

12. When done resting, place each Poffin, sealed side down, on the prepared baking sheet. Brush the Poffins with the egg wash and sprinkle the sesame seeds on top of each one.

13. Loosely cover the baking sheet with aluminum foil, to prevent browning, and bake for about 17 minutes, or until firm.

CHOCOLATE SALTY BALLS

SERVES 4–5

It might be debatable whether *South Park* is really "geeky," but I think the show has earned a lot of geek cred over the years with detailed references to such definitively geeky things as *World of Warcraft*, comic books, and *Star Trek*. *South Park* is generally not a good source of fictional food inspiration, as most of the satire is based in the real world and the show tends to aim for gross rather than appealing, but there is one exception: Chef's Chocolate Salty Balls.

Chef, voiced by the late Isaac Hayes, was the portly and promiscuous cafeteria cook for the first ten seasons of the show. As one of the kinder and more down-to-earth characters, his advice was often sought by the four protagonists . . . though his advice generally manifested itself in totally inappropriate and nonrelevant soul songs. This recipe comes from one of those humorously misguided soul songs, probably the most popular song from the show, titled "Chocolate Salty Balls." The song basically describes a recipe for a salty spherical chocolate pastry to . . . suck on. Despite the obvious metaphor here, I thought a salty spherical chocolate pastry sounded pretty darn good, and I was right! Chef's balls are delicious!

INGREDIENTS

Butter or nonstick spray, for
 greasing
⅔ cup (150 g) salted butter
1½ cups (150 g) sugar
¼ cup (60 ml) brandy
4 cups (700 g) semisweet
 chocolate chips, divided
2 teaspoons vanilla extract
4 eggs
1½ cups (180 g) flour
½ teaspoon baking soda
2 tablespoons ground
 cinnamon
½ teaspoon table salt
Coarse sea salt, to taste,
 for dusting

1. Preheat the oven to 325°F (170°C) and grease a baking pan.

2. In a saucepan, add the butter, sugar, and brandy, and bring to a boil, stirring constantly. Remove from the heat.

3. Using a wooden spoon, stir in 2 cups (350 g) of the chocolate chips until melted. Remember to give that spoon a lick! Allow the mixture to cool slightly, then stir in the vanilla extract.

4. In a large bowl, beat the eggs until combined. Gradually add the slightly cooled chocolate mixture and mix well.

5. Combine the flour, baking soda, cinnamon, and salt, then gradually add this mixture to the chocolate mixture.

6. Stir in the remaining 2 cups (350 g) chocolate chips and spread the mixture into the baking pan.

7. Bake for 35–45 minutes, or until a fork inserted in the center comes out clean. Be careful not to burn your balls!

8. Let the mixture cool just enough so that it won't burn your hands. Meanwhile, set up a small plate or cutting board with some sea salt on it.

9. Scrape up the baked chocolate, working around the edges—you don't want to use the hard edges for these balls.

10. Begin roughly shaping the baked chocolate into 1-inch (2.5 cm) balls, then roll them in the sea salt. Lightly do this—a little sea salt goes a long way.

11. If you do happen to oversalt, just brush off the excess crystals. Too much salt is bad, mmmkay? When you're done, put 'em in your mouth and suck 'em!

BUTTERSCOTCH CINNAMON PIE

SERVES 6–8

This one comes from a retro-style indie video game called *Undertale*. In *Undertale*, you control a small child who finds themself in a mysterious and occasionally hostile underground region where nothing is as it seems. *Undertale* is full of surprises and does a great job of turning a lot of video game tropes on their heads.

In the beginning of the game, you meet a kind soul named Toriel, who acts as your guide but must leave you for a while. Isn't that just like a video game guide? While you're adventuring by yourself, Toriel calls you on your cell phone and asks whether you prefer cinnamon or butterscotch, and you can choose whichever. After spending some time solving puzzles and complimenting frogs, you make your way to Toriel's very cozy home, where she has prepared a butterscotch *and* cinnamon pie for you. This was a fun recipe to create, it's stupid easy, and the end result is delicious. Enjoy this pie after a nice spaghetti dinner!

INGREDIENTS

1 Single-Crust Pie Dough
(page 13)

FILLING
1½ cups (350 ml) whole milk
½ cup (240 g) cream
⅔ cup (150 g) packed light
  brown sugar
¼ cup (32 g) cornstarch
½ teaspoon salt
½ teaspoon ground cinnamon
2 egg yolks, beaten
1 tablespoon unsalted butter
1 teaspoon vanilla extract

TOPPING
1 cup (120 g) heavy whipping
  cream
2 tablespoons granulated sugar
Ground cinnamon, for
  sprinkling

1. Preheat the oven to 375°F (190°C).

2. Using a pastry roller, roll out the dough to fit a 9-inch (23 cm) pie tin and press the dough evenly onto the bottom and sides of the tin. Cut off any excess.

3. Bake the crust by itself for 7 minutes. Remove from the oven and set aside.

4. **To make the filling:** In a double boiler, combine the milk, cream, brown sugar, cornstarch, salt, and cinnamon. Stir the mixture using a whisk and keep stirring until it thickens. If you don't have a double boiler, boil water in a saucepan and suspend a stainless steel or Pyrex bowl above it, so that no steam can escape. This will heat the contents of the bowl just right, without burning any of it.

5. Whisk the egg yolks into the mixture, still over the heat, pouring them in slowly. Continue to whisk constantly until the mixture thickens to almost the consistency of pudding. Remove from the heat, then add the butter and vanilla and stir some more, until both are completely incorporated.

6. Pour the mixture into the pie crust. Bake the pie for 7 minutes, then remove from the oven.

7. Let the pie cool for a few minutes on the counter and then transfer it to the fridge until it's at least at room temperature. When it's almost done cooling, prepare the topping.

8. **To make the topping:** Add the cream and sugar to a bowl, and whip with a hand mixer until it forms soft peaks. Be careful not to over-whip.

9. Spread the whipped cream on top of the chilled pie and sprinkle with the cinnamon.

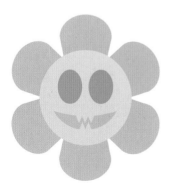

CHIMICHERRYCHANGA

MAKES 5 CHIMICHERRYCHANGAS

How did a show for little girls become a valid geeky interest for adults? I honestly don't know. Bronies are a strange and fascinating phenomenon. Far and away, I get more requests for *My Little Pony* recipes than from any other fandom. But I'm no neighsayer or parasprite, the love that these geeks have for this show is pure and unquestionable and I immensely respect it. You keep on doing you, bronies! Brohoof!

This little gem of a food concept appeared in the fourteenth episode of the second season called "The Last Roundup." While Applejack is away competing in a rodeo, the ponies receive a letter from Applejack saying she is not planning to return to Ponyville. The ponies immediately track her down to find out what happened, and when Applejack refuses to explain her reasoning, Pinkie Pie is sent to annoy Applejack into fessing up. During Pinkie Pie's relentless rambling, she discusses her idea to make a chimichanga filled with cherries and debates incessantly about whether the creations should be called Chimi-Cherries or Cherry-Changas. Luckily, I already have a killer dessert chimichanga recipe in my repertoire, so this is a modified version of that. It tastes pretty much like a churro stuffed with cherry cheesecake. Don't worry, it contains absolutely no oatmeal. . . . That would be crazy.

INGREDIENTS

8 ounces (227 g) cream cheese
½ cup (115 g) ricotta cheese
½ cup (115 g) sour cream
1 teaspoon vanilla extract
2 teaspoons lemon zest
Canola or vegetable oil, for
  deep-frying
5 large soft flour tortillas
½ cup (100 g) sugar
21 ounces (600 g) cherry filling
Cinnamon sugar, for coating

1. In a large bowl, combine the cream cheese, ricotta, sour cream, vanilla, and lemon zest using a mixer.

2. Heat the oil in a deep fryer or heavy-bottom pot to 340°F (170°C). If you do not have a candy thermometer, toss a piece of bread into the hot oil—if it turns golden in about 20 seconds, it's the right temperature. Add the fryer basket now, if you have one.

3. Warm the tortillas in the microwave for a few seconds to soften them. Evenly distribute the cheese mixture among the tortillas, spooning it into the center. Do the same with the cherry filling, spooning it on top of the cheese.

4. Tuck in the ends of the tortillas, then fold around the filling and roll. If you aren't great with burrito rolling, think of it like wrapping a present, but without tape.

5. Carefully set one of the ChimiCherryChangas in the hot oil. Fry for about 2 minutes or until it is golden brown. If you do not have a fryer basket, use tongs to gently remove it from the oil. Roll, brush, or sprinkle it with cinnamon sugar. Repeat for each Cherry-Changa. Or Chimi-Cherry. Or Cherry-Changa. Or Chimi-Cherry . . .

COOKIE CAT

MAKES 8 COOKIE CATS

Steven Universe was created by Rebecca Sugar of *Adventure Time* fame. It centers around the Crystal Gems, a group of extraterrestrial superheroes, and Steven, a half-human boy with powers he's only begun to explore. The series has been praised for its strong characterization and world-building, the latter of which uses elements of both fantasy and sci-fi.

These delicious pets for your tummy appeared in "Gem Glow," the very first episode of the series. In the episode, Steven discovers that Cookie Cats, his favorite ice-cream sandwich, have been discontinued and, unfortunately, that's not the only tragedy Beach City is facing. In the episode, Cookie Cats help Steven to defeat the giant evil eye heading for the town. Cookie Cats might just unlock your crystal powers, or inspire you to burst into song. Possibly both at once! They are so much better than Lion Lickers, which nobody really likes and don't even look like lions.

INGREDIENTS

1 pint (475 ml) strawberry and/
   or vanilla ice cream, softened
1 ⅓ cups (165 g) all-purpose
   flour, plus extra for dusting
¼ cup (27 g) unsweetened
   cocoa powder
1 teaspoon baking powder
⅛ teaspoon salt
⅓ cup (80 g) unsalted butter,
   softened
¾ cup (170 g) packed light
   brown sugar
1 tablespoon vanilla extract
2 eggs

1. The first thing you want to do is get a baking sheet that can fit in your freezer, then line it with parchment paper. Spoon and spread your ice cream into an even layer on the baking sheet. If you're using both strawberry and vanilla ice cream, do this in alternating lines. Cover with plastic wrap and freeze overnight.

2. In a bowl, sift the flour, cocoa powder, baking powder, and salt. Set aside.

3. In a separate large bowl, use a mixer to cream together the butter and brown sugar for about 1 minute, or until completely mixed. Turn the mixer to medium-low and add the vanilla extract and the eggs, then beat until the eggs and extract are incorporated, about 1 minute.

4. Add the dry ingredients to the wet ingredients. Mix on medium-low for about 1 minute. Everything should be completely incorporated at this point and the dough should be soft and sticky.

5. Lightly dust a work surface with flour and place the dough on it. Work the dough into a ½-inch-thick (13 mm) flat circle. Wrap the dough in plastic wrap and refrigerate for at least 1 hour, or until it's firm enough to roll out.

6. Once the dough is firmed up, dust your work surface, the dough, and your rolling pin with flour. Roll out the dough to between ⅛ and ¼ inch (3 and 6 mm) thick.

7. It's actually fairly easy to create the cat shape. Make a template for yourself using paper or cardboard. Draw a wide oval and add two triangular ears on top. Use scissors to cut out the template and place it over the edge of the rolled-out dough. Use a sharp knife to carefully cut the dough around the edges of the template. You can use a soda or water bottle to stamp out the eyes, and you only need to make eye holes for half the cookies.

8. Carefully transfer the cut cookies to a parchment-lined baking sheet. Gather the scraps, work and roll the dough again, then cut out the remaining cookies until you have 16 total. Dust with flour as needed. Place the cut cookies in the refrigerator for 20–30 minutes, which will prevent the cookies from spreading too much and becoming misshapen.

9. Preheat the oven to 350°F (180°C) with a baking rack placed in the center. Bake the cookies for 11–12 minutes. They will still feel soft when done, and that's okay. Carefully transfer to a rack to cool completely.

10. Once the cookies are cool and firm, get out your sheet of ice cream. Use the cat template to cut out the cat shape in the ice cream. Place this on top of one of the eyeless cookies, then add one of the cookies with eyes on top. Repeat until all the cookies are used. Chill the completed cookies in your special freezer for at least 20 minutes before serving. They'll keep for about a week.

LINGONBERRY PANCAKES

MAKES 15 PANCAKES

The Big Lebowski is easily the most quoted Coen Brothers' film. It stars Jeff Bridges, who many of us geeks will remember as the guy from the original *Tron*, but many more folks know him as The Dude. The Dude's adventures begin when his home is invaded by a couple of thugs who've mistaken him for someone else: a wealthy man who shares his name, Jeffrey Lebowski. The Dude decides to visit this other Lebowski and demand he pay for the damages to his apartment, particularly his defiled rug. That's when things go wrong.

Lingonberry Pancakes appeared in a scene toward the end of the film. You may recall the scene as the one that made you go "OMG is that Aimee Mann and Flea?!" While in a diner, the German Nihilists all order Lingonberry Pancakes, except for Flea, who orders "Pigs in Blanket." Actually, Aimee Mann orders "Heidelbeerpfannkuchen," which is blueberry pancakes in German, but it is incorrectly translated to Lingonberry Pancakes by her boyfriend. Wash these delicious babies down with a White Russian* . . . unless you don't like White Russians, then, well, The Dude does not abide.

* For those who don't know, a "White Russian" is vodka, coffee liqueur, and cream, typically at a 5:2:3 ratio.

INGREDIENTS

2 eggs
2 cups (475 ml) milk
1¼ cups (155 g) all-purpose flour
¼ cup (50 g) granulated sugar
Pinch salt
¼ cup or ½ stick (60 g) unsalted butter, melted
Vegetable oil or butter, for frying
Lingonberry preserves, to taste (you can buy this online or at Ikea)
Confectioners' sugar, for serving
Whipped cream, for serving

1. Beat the eggs in a medium bowl until foamy. Add the milk, flour, sugar, and salt, stirring until fully mixed. Lastly, stir in the melted butter.

2. Cover the batter with plastic wrap and refrigerate for at least 2 hours, but overnight is better.

3. Heat some vegetable oil or butter over medium-high heat in a skillet or griddle. Pour a thin stream of batter into a circular shape onto the hot griddle or skillet, keeping in mind that the pancakes should be 5–6 inches (13–15 cm) in diameter and very thin. Cook the pancake on one side for 20 seconds, flip, and cook on the other side for 20 seconds until done. Set the cooked pancake aside and repeat until you have about 15 pancakes, adding more oil or butter as needed to prevent sticking.

4. Spread the lingonberry preserves in the center of a pancake, then roll the pancake up around the preserves so they're tube-shaped. Repeat for each pancake.

5. Sprinkle the completed pancakes with the confectioners' sugar and top with the whipped cream.

NONFAT TOFUTTI RICE DREAMSICLE

MAKES 1 QUART OR 2 PINTS

The X-Files dominated the '90s geek scene. It somehow made extraterrestrial conspiracy theories cool. The dynamic between believer Mulder and skeptical Scully is now the stuff of legends. During their search for the truth, there have been some rare food moments. Like that one time when Scully was somehow still dignified and sexy with a face covered in barbecue sauce and stuffing ribs into her mouth—one of the many reasons Scully is my hero.

This little gem appears in a delightful scene from the season 6 episode "The Unnatural," in which Mulder teases Scully about her frozen dessert and life choices. So, we have some clues about what's going on with this "ice cream" abomination: there's tofu, rice, and orange-vanilla flavor served in a cone. Unfortunately, it's impossible to make this truly "nonfat." I've never seen nonfat tofu. Despite this, or probably because of it, the recipe actually results in some pretty tasty vegan ice cream. This is just speculation, but I'm pretty sure that, despite his assertions otherwise, it tastes significantly better than the air in Mulder's mouth, though I'm sure some of us wouldn't mind testing that particular theory!

INGREDIENTS

EQUIPMENT
Ice cream maker

"ICE CREAM"
16 ounces (454 g) silken tofu
2¼ cups (540 ml) vanilla rice milk
¼ cup (90 g) agave nectar, or more
1 teaspoon orange extract
½ teaspoon vanilla extract
1½ teaspoons xanthan gum
Sugar waffle cones, for serving

1. Blend all the ingredients—except for the xanthan gum and waffle cones—in a blender.

2. While the blender is blending, slowly sprinkle in the xanthan gum.

3. When the base is smooth and creamy, pour it into a container and place in the fridge until the ingredients are cold, about 2 hours (this timing depends on your fridge, the initial temperature of the ingredients, and so on).

4. Use the base according to your ice-cream maker's instructions.

5. Freeze for 30 minutes before scooping into the waffle cone.

INDEX

Cassandra Reeder is an experienced blogger, avid home cook, and lifetime geek. For over a decade she has been helping other geeks all over the world make their fictional food fantasies come true at www.geekychef.com. She is also the author of *The Geeky Chef Strikes Back* and *The Geeky Chef Drinks*. Cassandra currently lives and cooks in Portland, Oregon, with her husband, son, and a magical talking parrot.